SAVING ENDANGERED SPECIES

THE
HUMPBACK
WHALE

Help Save This Endangered Species!

Deborah Kops

MyReportLinks.com Books

an imprint of

Enslow Publishers, Inc.

Box 398, 40 Industrial Road
Berkeley Heights, NJ 07922
USA

For Noah, Ben, and Jonah

MyReportLinks.com Books, an imprint of Enslow Publishers, Inc. MyReportLinks®
is a registered trademark of Enslow Publishers, Inc.

Library of Congress Cataloging-in-Publication Data

Kops, Deborah.
  The humpback whale: help save this endangered species! / Deborah Kops.
    p. cm. — (Saving endangered species)
  Includes bibliographical references.
  ISBN 1-59845-036-0
  1. Humpback whale—Juvenile literature. I. Title. II. Series.
  QL737.C424K67 2006
  599.5'25—dc22

                    2005017340

Printed in the United States of America

10 9 8 7 6 5 4 3 2 1

To Our Readers:
Through the purchase of this book, you and your library gain access to the Report Links that specifically
back up this book.
The Publisher will provide access to the Report Links that back up this book and will keep these Report
Links up to date on **www.myreportlinks.com** for five years from the book's first publication date.
We have done our best to make sure all Internet addresses in this book were active and appropriate when
we went to press. However, the author and the Publisher have no control over, and assume no liability
for, the material available on those Internet sites or on other Web sites they may link to.
The usage of the MyReportLinks.com Books Web site is subject to the terms and conditions stated on the
Usage Policy Statement on **www.myreportlinks.com**.
A password may be required to access the Report Links that back up this book. The password is found
on the bottom of page 4 of this book.
Any comments or suggestions can be sent by e-mail to comments@myreportlinks.com or to the address
on the back cover.

Photo Credits: © Corel Corporation, pp. 25, 78, 89, 104; American Cetacean Society, p. 71; Captain
Bud Christman, NOAA, pp. 86–87; Caroline Theberge, NOAA, p. 12; Cetacea.org, p. 63; Commander
John Bortniak, NOAA, p. 10; Enslow Publishers, Inc., pp. 1, 3, 5–7; EPA, p. 62; Greenpeace, p. 65;
Hawaiian Islands Humpback Whale National Marine Sanctuary, p. 75; International Whaling
Commission, p. 69; Library of Congress, pp. 46, 72; Marine Science, p. 51; Monterey Bay NMS, p. 17;
MyReportLinks.com Books, p. 4; National Marine Fisheries Service, p. 103; National Marine Mammal
Laboratory, p. 94; National Wildlife Federation, p. 96; New Bedford Whaling Museum, p. 49; NOAA,
pp. 1, 3, 15, 28–29, 34, 47, 58, 61, 92, 113; NSW National Parks and Wildlife Service, p. 23; Ocean
Alliance, p. 35; Pacific Whale Foundation, p. 91; PBS, pp. 20, 110; Photos.com, pp. 27, 32, 54–55;
Provincetown Center for Coastal Studies, p. 98; SeaWorld, p. 22; Species at Risk, p. 37; Stellwagen Bank
National Marine Sanctuary, p. 82; The Marine Mammal Center, p. 101; The Oceania Project, p. 42;
University of California, p. 53; USFWS, pp. 14, 115; Whale and Dolphin Conservation Society, p. 107;
Whale Center of New England, p. 84; Whale Songs, p. 100; WWF, p. 76.

Cover Photo: Painet Stock Photos.

CONTENTS

MyReportLinks.com Books
Great Books, Great Links, Great for Research!

The Internet sites featured in this book can save you hours of research time. These Internet sites—we call them **"Report Links"**—are constantly changing, but we keep them up to date on our Web site.

When you see this "Approved Web Site" logo, you will know that we are directing you to a great Internet site that will help you with your research.

Give it a try! Type **http://www.myreportlinks.com** into your browser, click on the series title and enter the password, then click on the book title, and scroll down to the Report Links listed for this book.

The Report Links will bring you to great source documents, photographs, and illustrations. MyReportLinks.com Books save you time, feature Report Links that are kept up to date, and make report writing easier than ever! A complete listing of the Report Links can be found on pages 116–117 at the back of the book.

Please see "To Our Readers" on the copyright page for important information about this book, the MyReportLinks.com Web site, and the Report Links that back up this book.

Please enter **SHW1162** if asked for a password.

The Humpback Whale
Range Map

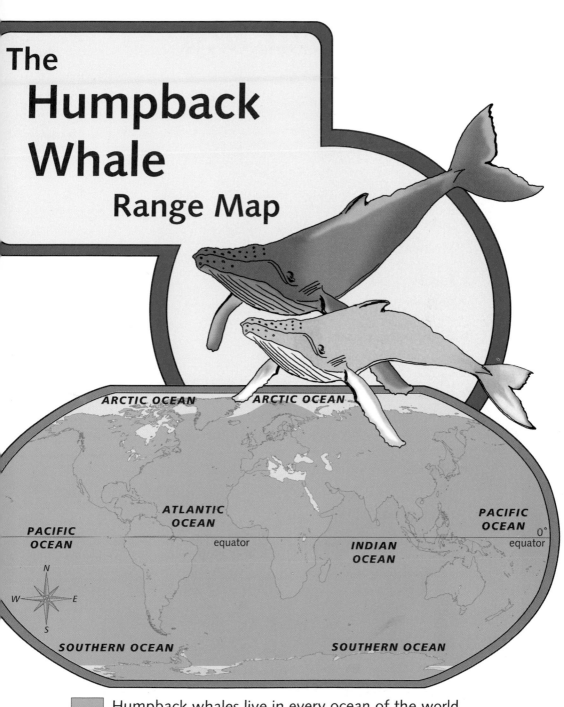

ARCTIC OCEAN   ARCTIC OCEAN

ATLANTIC
OCEAN

PACIFIC
OCEAN   equator

PACIFIC
OCEAN   0°

                INDIAN
                OCEAN   equator

N
W   E
S

SOUTHERN OCEAN   SOUTHERN OCEAN

Humpback whales live in every ocean of the world. Most populations spend winters in warm tropical waters near the equator.

Humpback Whale Facts

▶ **Class**

Mammalia

▶ **Order**

Cetacea

▶ **Suborder**

Mysticeti

▶ **Family**

Balaenopteridae

▶ **Genus and Species**

Megaptera novaeangliae

▶ **Estimated Population**

Although estimates vary, some scientists think there are between 25,000 and 30,000 humpbacks worldwide.

▶ **Status**

The humpback whale is currently listed as endangered throughout its entire range.

▶ **Distinct Population Groups**

There are four populations of humpbacks worldwide: the North Pacific, North Atlantic, South Atlantic, and Indian Ocean.

▶ **Length**

Males are 35 to 45 feet (11 to 14 meters); females are 45 to 55 feet (14 to 17 meters).

▶ **Weight**

Between 25 and 40 tons (23 and 36 metric tons)

▶ Skin Color

Black on top and black and white on the underside

▶ Fin, Flippers, and Flukes

Humpbacks have an irregularly shaped dorsal fin; flippers that are between one quarter and one third the length of the whale's body; and powerful flukes that can measure 18 feet (5.5 meters).

▶ Teeth

500 to 800 individual baleen plates hanging from the roof of the mouth

▶ Number of Blowholes

Two

▶ Length of Dive

Three to ten minutes, but may be up to thirty minutes

▶ Age at Sexual Maturity

Between four and seven years of age

▶ Gestation

Twelve months

▶ Life Span

The average life span is unknown but is thought to be between fifty and sixty years.

▶ Range

There are humpbacks in every ocean in the world. Most populations spend summers in cold ocean waters and winters in tropical waters closer to the equator.

▶ Threats to Survival

Whale hunting, entanglement in fishing equipment, collisions with ships, ocean pollution, and global warming

Found in all the world's oceans, the Humpback Whale is a truly magnificent animal, the acrobat of the great whale species and a fine singer.

Mark Simmonds, *Whales and Dolphins of the World,* 2004

HUMPBACKS NEED OUR HELP

On a fall day in Alaska in 2001, a man was out in his boat in Resurrection Bay, a scenic body of water surrounded by mountains. There, on the bay, he spotted a young humpback whale dragging a strange, heavy load: a thirty-pound anchor, a crab pot for catching crabs, some chain, three buoys, and two plastic foam floats. (A buoy is a colorful marker made out of wood or Styrofoam that floats on the water and helps fishermen find their crab or lobster traps.) This jumble of fishing gear was tangled with ropes, which the whale had accidentally caught in its mouth.

The man in the boat called for help. Within hours, a rescue team arrived on the scene in a small inflatable boat. The rescuers were from the United States Coast Guard, the National Marine Fisheries Service (NMFS), which is part of the National Oceanic and Atmospheric Administration, or NOAA, and the Alaska SeaLife Center in Seward.

The rescuers cautiously approached the whale and put the buoys in their boat. The buoys were

Humpbacks, like this one breaching, can be found in every ocean of the world. It is up to us to make sure that this majestic species survives.

attached to the tangled ropes, and the ropes were attached at the other end to the whale's mouth. Slowly the rescuers began pulling the ropes into the boat, which gradually brought them closer to the whale. Since it was a young humpback, it was only about twenty feet (six meters) long. *Only?* Actually, that is about the length of three long dining tables placed end to end.

For two hours, the rescuers pulled the rope into the boat, cutting it off in lengths. Eventually the whale only had a short piece in its mouth, which the rescuers left for the whale to get rid of. The whale took a deep dive before heading in the direction of the wide-open waters of the Gulf of Alaska.

The young whale was lucky. It was not badly injured and only had some scrapes around its mouth.[1] Its predicament was not unusual, however. These whales share the sea with fishermen, and they often become tangled in fishermen's gear. Sometimes they disentangle themselves, sometimes they are rescued, and sometimes, unfortunately, they die.

Humpback whales swim in every ocean in the world.[2] From Australia to Cape Cod, Massachusetts, thousands of people go on whale-watching trips to observe these huge marine mammals, hoping to see them breach, or leap out of the water. Of all the large whales, humpbacks are the greatest acrobats. They turn whale watchers into whale lovers.

Why Humpbacks Are Endangered

Many whales, both juvenile and mature, become tangled in fishing gear like the young humpback. Fishing nets and crab and lobster pots are a serious problem, but they did not bring the humpbacks close to extinction. Whaling did.

Humans have been hunting whales for thousands of years, eating the whale's meat and using other parts of its body for oil, clothing, and shelter. Many researchers guess there were about 150,000 humpbacks before people hunted whales.[3]

▲ *This humpback in the waters off Cape Cod appears to be waving to the photographer. Humpbacks are among the most acrobatic of whales.*

Humpbacks first received protection in 1963 through the International Whaling Commission (IWC), an organization founded in 1946 to conserve whale stocks so that whaling could continue. In the United States, humpbacks were listed as an endangered species, a species at risk of going extinct, in 1970. But even with these protections, illegal whaling continued, and by the mid-1980s, there were only about 25,000 humpbacks left. In 1986, the IWC put a moratorium, a temporary halt, into effect that stopped almost all whaling throughout the world.

Since the IWC declared the moratorium on whaling, humpback populations in some parts of the world have been increasing. A few countries would like to begin hunting whales again, however. Humpbacks face other threats, too, including ocean pollution and even noise pollution. (Whales may be affected by loud noises since they rely upon sound for communication and location.) Global warming is another problem. It is the result of a buildup of harmful gases in the earth's atmosphere and may be raising the temperature of the oceans and melting some of the ice at the North and South Poles. The melting ice shelves may in turn affect the humpbacks' food supply. Although researchers disagree about how global warming will affect humpbacks, there is no disagreement about a more concrete danger. Large ships on the high seas sometimes accidentally hit whales, including humpbacks.

▶ You Can Help Save Humpbacks

Around the world, conservationists, scientists, researchers, and government officials are involved in efforts to save humpbacks and other endangered marine mammals. But their efforts will mean little if the rest of us do not do our part to protect our planet's wildlife and wild places. There are many things that *you* can do right now to help.

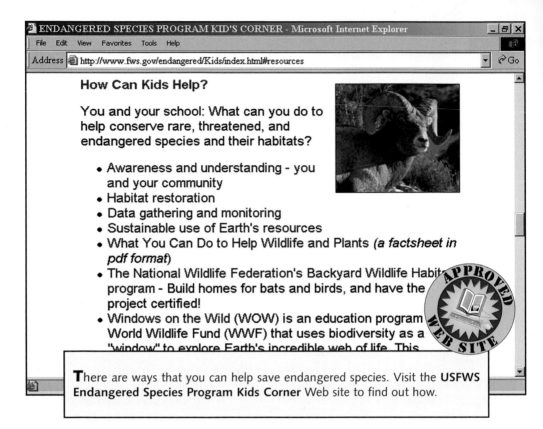

ENDANGERED SPECIES PROGRAM KID'S CORNER - Microsoft Internet Explorer

File   Edit   View   Favorites   Tools   Help

Address http://www.fws.gov/endangered/Kids/index.html#resources

How Can Kids Help?

You and your school: What can you do to help conserve rare, threatened, and endangered species and their habitats?

- Awareness and understanding - you and your community
- Habitat restoration
- Data gathering and monitoring
- Sustainable use of Earth's resources
- What You Can Do to Help Wildlife and Plants (*a factsheet in pdf format*)
- The National Wildlife Federation's Backyard Wildlife Habitat program - Build homes for bats and birds, and have the project certified!
- Windows on the Wild (WOW) is an education program World Wildlife Fund (WWF) that uses biodiversity as a "window" to explore Earth's incredible web of life. This

There are ways that you can help save endangered species. Visit the **USFWS Endangered Species Program Kids Corner** Web site to find out how.

First and foremost, learn as much as you can about humpback whales. The Web sites of whale research and conservation organizations are a good place to start. Some of them offer individuals and groups the chance to "adopt" a whale through a donation. Under your teacher's supervision, you and the other members of your class could hold a fund-raising event and donate the proceeds to an organization that is working to protect whales and their habitat.

For more in-depth knowledge, ask your teacher or school librarian to recommend books about whales and marine mammal conservation. The more you know about humpbacks (and other endangered animals), the more likely you are to care about them—and about what will happen to these creatures if we allow them to disappear from the earth forever. Then share that knowledge with others.

Cruising for Conservation

One of the most exciting ways to learn about whales is to go on a whale watch. If you live or vacation where whales are, take a cruise from a

http://www.sanctuaries.nos.noaa.gov/pgallery/pgstellwagen/human/whalewatch_300.jpg - Microsoft Intern...

File Edit View Favorites Tools Help

Address http://www.sanctuaries.nos.noaa.gov/pgallery/pgstellwagen/human/whalewatch_300.jpg

The people aboard this whale-watching cruise in the Stellwagen Bank National Marine Sanctuary are treated to the sight of a breaching humpback. At NOAA's **National Marine Sanctuaries** Web site, learn more about these federally protected places.

responsible company. Ask if it obeys the speed limits recommended by the National Marine Fisheries Service. These boats are much less likely to hit a whale by accident, and responsible cruises will not approach a whale too closely.

If you are close enough to a diving humpback, take a picture of its flukes, or tail. Then send the photo to the nearest conservation organization for marine mammals. They may be able to identify the humpback from the unique pattern on its tail and gain some useful information about its travels.

If you are out on the ocean in a private boat with your family and you see a whale entangled in fishing gear, ask an adult to call the Coast Guard. It will notify a rescue team. After calling the Coast Guard, the most helpful thing you and your family can do is try to keep the whale in sight, but do not venture too close, since you may make the situation worse. Once the rescue boat finds you, it will be able to find the whale.[4]

▶ Saving Our Oceans

You can also help whales by making sure that your actions do not harm their habitat—the world's oceans. One way to do this is to help slow global warming by cutting car emissions. If you carpool with a friend to your soccer or baseball game, you and your friend are cutting back on pollution in the air just by using one car instead of two. If you

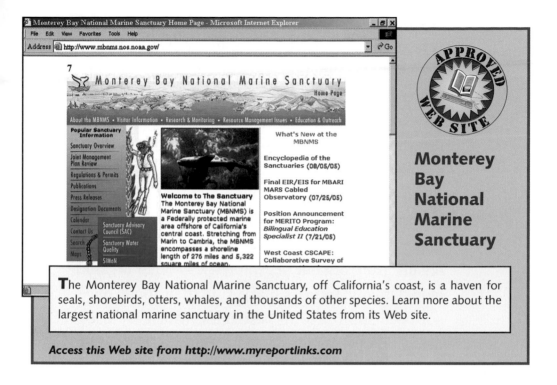

The Monterey Bay National Marine Sanctuary, off California's coast, is a haven for seals, shorebirds, otters, whales, and thousands of other species. Learn more about the largest national marine sanctuary in the United States from its Web site.

Access this Web site from http://www.myreportlinks.com

are waiting in a car on a hot day, step outside and get some fresh air. That is much better for the atmosphere than asking your mom or dad to keep the air conditioning on, because the motor has to be on, too. Keeping an engine idling is more polluting to the atmosphere than starting up a car. Even better, walk or ride a bicycle instead of jumping into a car for a short trip—that way, the air will stay cleaner and you will be fitter.

To help keep the ocean waters clean, recycle as much as possible. Plastic bottles and containers that find their way into the ocean float on the water. Marine mammals, including whales, sometimes swallow them and can choke. When you are at the beach, be especially careful to dispose of your trash properly. If you are lucky enough to live in a coastal community, organize a beach cleanup. Closer to home, ask your parents not to use fertilizers and insecticides on your lawn, or at least to use those products sparingly. When it rains, the chemicals in them are washed into streams and rivers and eventually make their way into our oceans, which is where whales make their home.

You can also encourage your parents to buy organic fruit, organic vegetables, and other organic food. Organic farmers make sure their foods have not been sprayed with pesticides, which are used to get rid of agricultural pests. Harmful chemicals in these sprays end up in the oceans just as the chemicals in lawn products do. In addition to benefiting the ocean, organic products are better for you, too.

THE GIANT SINGER OF THE SEA

In 1970, before people had CD players, Capitol Records pressed 10 million copies of a very unusual record. Produced in cooperation with the National Geographic Society, it was the largest pressing in recording history. The recording artists had never made a record before. In fact, they were not human; they were male humpbacks! The *Songs of the Humpback Whale* was a huge hit.

Do male humpbacks really sing? Researchers believe they do. On the recording, the humpback "music" sounds like a series of snores, whistles, and eerie noises like a cow mooing in an echo chamber.[1] Although the music is strange to human ears, the patterns of humpback songs are similar to music composed by people: In one section of a song, you can hear a theme. Then the whale develops and changes it. Finally, the "singer" returns to the original theme. Each song, always produced by a male, lasts about fifteen to twenty minutes. Humpbacks will sing for hours, though.

▶ "An Exuberant River of Sound"

Roger Payne, an expert on whales and one of the scientists who first discovered the humpback's musical talents, described a humpback concert: "A long singing session is an exuberant, uninterrupted river of sound that can flow on for twenty-four hours or longer. The pace of the [singing] is very grand and extended and appears to me to be set by the slow rhythm of the ocean swells—the rhythm of the sea."[2]

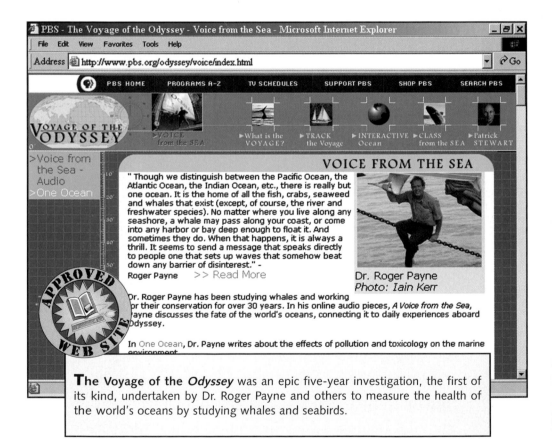

PBS - The Voyage of the Odyssey - Voice from the Sea - Microsoft Internet Explorer

File   Edit   View   Favorites   Tools   Help

Address http://www.pbs.org/odyssey/voice/index.html   Go

PBS HOME   PROGRAMS A-Z   TV SCHEDULES   SUPPORT PBS   SHOP PBS   SEARCH PBS

VOYAGE OF THE
ODYSSEY   ▶VOICE   ▶What is the   ▶TRACK   ▶INTERACTIVE   ▶CLASS   ▶Patrick
            from the SEA   VOYAGE?   the Voyage   Ocean   from the SEA   STEWART

>Voice from
the Sea -
Audio
>One Ocean

VOICE FROM THE SEA

" Though we distinguish between the Pacific Ocean, the Atlantic Ocean, the Indian Ocean, etc., there is really but one ocean. It is the home of all the fish, crabs, seaweed and whales that exist (except, of course, the river and freshwater species). No matter where you live along any seashore, a whale may pass along your coast, or come into any harbor or bay deep enough to float it. And sometimes they do. When that happens, it is always a thrill. It seems to send a message that speaks directly to people one that sets up waves that somehow beat down any barrier of disinterest." -
Roger Payne   >> Read More

Dr. Roger Payne
Photo: Iain Kerr

Dr. Roger Payne has been studying whales and working for their conservation for over 30 years. In his online audio pieces, *A Voice from the Sea*, Payne discusses the fate of the world's oceans, connecting it to daily experiences aboard Odyssey.

In One Ocean, Dr. Payne writes about the effects of pollution and toxicology on the marine environment.

The Voyage of the *Odyssey* was an epic five-year investigation, the first of its kind, undertaken by Dr. Roger Payne and others to measure the health of the world's oceans by studying whales and seabirds.

Only male whales sing, in a set pattern of sounds called vocalizations. Humpbacks produce a wide and complex range of musical sounds. Researchers are not sure what humpbacks are communicating to one another with their songs, although many think that the songs are a way for the males to attract females. The songs of the humpbacks are intriguing for another reason: The whales in each population sing the same song, but that song differs from the songs of every other population, and each song changes a little year by year.

Humpbacks and Their Relatives

Humpback whales, like all whales, are mammals, which means they share many traits with other mammals, including humans. Humpbacks are warm-blooded, like people. Instead of laying eggs, like fish, whale mothers give birth to live young, which the mothers nourish with their milk. And humpbacks need to breathe in air, just as we do.

Humpbacks are members of the order Cetacea. This large group of marine mammals includes more than eighty kinds of whales, dolphins, and porpoises.[3] They range in size from the bottlenose dolphin to the blue whale, which is the largest animal on earth.

Whales are grouped into two main categories: those with teeth, known as toothed whales, and those with baleen plates, like the humpback, called

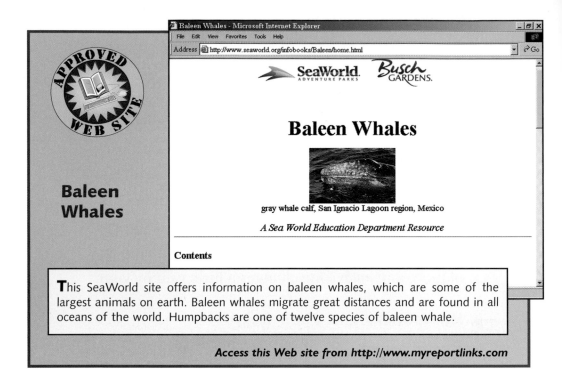

Baleen Whales - Microsoft Internet Explorer

File   Edit   View   Favorites   Tools   Help

Address   http://www.seaworld.org/infobooks/Baleen/home.html

SeaWorld. ADVENTURE PARKS   Busch GARDENS.

Baleen Whales

gray whale calf, San Ignacio Lagoon region, Mexico

A Sea World Education Department Resource

Contents

Baleen Whales

This SeaWorld site offers information on baleen whales, which are some of the largest animals on earth. Baleen whales migrate great distances and are found in all oceans of the world. Humpbacks are one of twelve species of baleen whale.

Access this Web site from http://www.myreportlinks.com

baleen whales. Baleen whales have hundreds of baleen plates hanging from the roof of their mouths, like a set of blinds, to help them filter their food. These plates also keep the whales from taking in too much salt water, which would lead to dehydration. Some baleen whales, including humpbacks, belong to a family of whales known as rorquals. Rorquals have a series of pleats, or grooves, that run from their throats to their flippers. These grooves expand when the whale eats. A rorqual also has a dorsal fin, a fin on its back, which helps to stabilize the whale when it makes sudden turns.

The Body of a Humpback

Humpbacks are large whales. Males can be 45 feet long (14 meters), and females are even longer— up to 55 feet (17 meters). That is about the length of three average-size cars. Adult humpbacks can weigh as much as 40 tons (36 metric tons), which is about the weight of seven elephants.

This whale is not an especially beautiful animal when it is resting. Its wide head and its lower jaw are covered with very small lumps. Often, its lower jaw is also home to a scattering of barnacles,

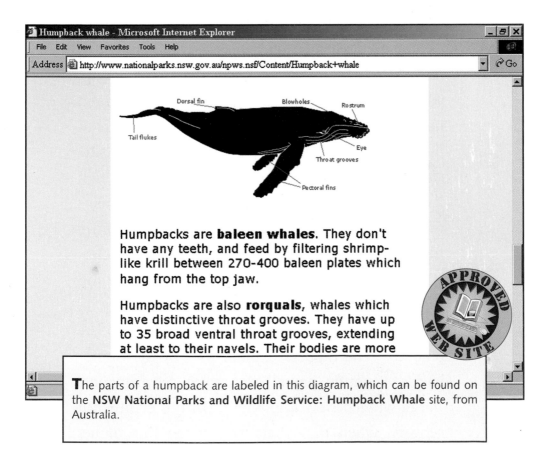

The parts of a humpback are labeled in this diagram, which can be found on the **NSW National Parks and Wildlife Service: Humpback Whale** site, from Australia.

which are white, hard-shelled creatures that attach themselves to the whale.

Humpbacks are black on top and a mixture of white and black underneath. Like all cetaceans, they have a layer of fat, called blubber, beneath their skin. Blubber keeps them warm when they are in very cold water. It also stores energy, which the humpbacks use during the long periods of time that they go without food.

▶ What's in a Name?

Humpbacks are known for their acrobatic dives. When it wants to go down deep into the water, a humpback arches its back before it dives. In this position, the whale's back looks like a large hump, which is probably how the whale got its common name. Humpbacks have two long, slim flippers at their sides, which they use to steer. These flippers can be up to 18 feet (5.5 meters) long and weigh 2,000 pounds (907 kilograms) each, which makes them the largest flippers of any whale. Sometimes from a distance, all you may see of a humpback is one long, winglike flipper, waving lazily back and forth. It looks, according to Roger Payne, "like an immense palm frond [leaf] bending slowly in the breeze."[4] The flippers explain part of the humpback's scientific name, *Megaptera novaeangliae*, "large-winged New Englander." In the eighteenth century, when the whale was given this name,

▲ Humpbacks have larger pectoral fins, or flippers, than any other whale species.

there were many more humpbacks swimming off the coast of New England than there are now.

Like all whales, a humpback has a tail that consists of two identical parts called flukes. On the underside of its flukes, each humpback has a slightly different black-and-white pattern, just as each person has a slightly different fingerprint. When the whale dives and its flukes shoot out of the water, it is easy to see the pattern. Researchers sometimes take pictures of a humpback's flukes to identify it.

Breathing, Diving, and Resting

Like all baleen whales, humpbacks have two blowholes. (Toothed whales have only one.) Since the blowholes are at the top of its head, the humpback can continue swimming while it breathes. To breathe, the humpback exhales, or breathes out, first. It opens its blowholes and lets out a column of gases from its lungs. The gases mix with the moisture in the air, resulting in a misty spray that boaters can see from a distance. This mist is called the whale's blow.

Immediately after it blows, a humpback breathes in air through its blowholes, filling its lungs. Then it quickly closes its blowholes and dives under water until it needs to breathe again. A humpback usually takes a series of breaths every three to ten minutes, but it can go thirty minutes

The blow of a humpback is made up of exhaled gases that mix with the moisture in the air to create a misty column.

without breathing if it must.[5] Some whales and dolphins can stay under water much longer. The champion is the sperm whale, which regularly spends about twenty to thirty minutes submerged at a time, searching for giant squid deep in the ocean.[6]

Like all mammals, humpbacks need to rest. They lie, stretched out, near the surface of the water, swimming occasionally.[7] But they do not fall asleep completely, as humans do. Humpbacks need to remain partially awake in order to breathe. Breathing is voluntary for whales. They need to think about every breath they take. For humans, breathing is involuntary, or automatic.

▶ The Humpback's Diet

Humpbacks are piscivores, animals that eat fish. The fish they eat are small, so they must eat lots

▲ Humpbacks lunge feeding: The whales take in huge gulps of water and large amounts of krill with it.

of them. Like other large whales, humpbacks eat the most in spring and summer to add to their blubber and store energy for their long trip to their winter grounds. But they also feed well into the fall, and some even feed into December.

Humpbacks eat a variety of fish, including anchovy, mackerel, cod, and herring. They also fill themselves with zooplankton, tiny animals that the whales consume in huge gulps.

Krill, a tiny shrimplike creature, is one kind of zooplankton that feeds thousands of humpbacks and other baleen whales. (Fish and seals like krill, too.) In the ocean between Australia and Antarctica, humpbacks sometimes feast on schools of krill that are miles wide and hundreds of feet deep.[8] A large group of whales may gather where the krill is swarming and eat for hours. They are not exactly delicate eaters. They make social

noises as they gulp their food, which attracts still more humpbacks to the swarm.

To catch a mass of prey, a humpback often lunge feeds. It swims into the mass with its mouth open so that gallons of water, with lots of prey swimming in it, rushes in. The whale's throat grooves expand like a balloon to make room for all of the water. Then the whale closes its mouth most of the way and forces the water out through its baleen plates. The baleen catch the zooplankton or small fish, and the water escapes through a gap between the whale's jaws.

▷ Other Feeding Techniques

Humpbacks have at least three other feeding techniques. One is called bubble netting. In this technique, the humpbacks position themselves below a swarm of krill or fish. Then they swim upward in a spiral pattern while blowing bubbles through their blowholes. Since the air bladders of fish and krill cannot deal with the change in pressure, they will not cross a train of bubbles. Trapped by the bubbles, they gather in great big schools, forming tasty mouthfuls of food for the humpbacks. Humpbacks may use bubble netting to feed cooperatively, or they may bubble net individually.

In 1981, researchers from the Whale Center of New England, in Massachusetts, noticed a feeding technique in New England waters that they had not seen before. Among some humpbacks that were bubble netting, one whale was adding her own touch. The researchers knew this whale and had named her Molson. She was slamming her tail down on the water, probably to surprise her prey and stop them right where they were. Then she dove beneath them, blew some bubbles at them, and took a great big gulp.

When the humpbacks returned the next spring, the researchers noticed that another humpback was using Molson's tail-slamming technique. By the end of the 1980s, the researchers were amazed to see that more than half of the humpbacks that fed in the region were slamming their tails when they ate.

The Whale Center staff noticed another feeding technique: bottom feeding. In New England, one of the small fish that humpbacks eat is the sand lance. These fish tend to gather together on the ocean bottom and will sometimes burrow into the sand for protection. The humpbacks brush the bottom of the seabed with their lower jaw so that the sand lances will swim up from the seabed, making them available to the whales. It is easy to tell which humpbacks do a lot of bottom feeding: They tend to have scratches on their lower jaw from rubbing against the sandy bottom of the sea.

▷ Breaching and Spyhopping

When children and adults climb eagerly aboard a whale-watching boat, they hope to see at least one whale—but not just in the water. A whale swimming by the boat may look like a giant log, but a

▲ *Its powerful flukes propel the humpback as it bursts from the sea when breaching.*

whale jumping all the way out of the water is a thrilling sight. This jump is called a breach.

Humpbacks are champions at breaching. After making a few powerful sweeps in the water with their flukes, they leap high out of the sea. For a moment they seem to hang suspended in the air. Then they come crashing back into the water on their sides, or they may do a spin before reentering the ocean. No one is sure why humpbacks breach, but some researchers believe that the whales' primary reason for breaching is to make a loud sound that acts as a warning, so that other males will stay away. Young humpbacks, on the other hand, seem to breach for the pleasure of it.[9]

People on a whale-watching boat are probably surprised by another whale behavior called spy-hopping. Humpbacks are curious. Sometimes they want to get a good look at a boat full of whale watchers or something else that interests them. They poke their heads above the water, like a person treading water. Sometimes they turn all the way around. But this behavior is not common.

The Southern Humpback's Long Journeys of Migration

As spring arrives in Antarctica, the days, which were so short and dark in winter, grow longer and brighter. Much of Antarctica is always covered by two huge sheets of ice called ice shelves. In spring and summer, big blocks of ice separate from the ice shelves and float into the surrounding Southern Ocean. Masses of packed sea ice begin to melt. The melting and increased sunlight cause tiny plants known as phytoplankton that were under the sea

▲ *With a boat in the distant background, this humpback takes a peek above water, in a behavior known as spyhopping.*

ice during the winter to multiply in the ocean. Krill hatch from eggs and eat the tiny plants.

The Southern Ocean is the spring and summer feeding grounds for thousands of humpbacks. Some migrate from the waters around Australia. Others make the trip from the waters around the South Pacific island of Fiji, about three thousand miles (forty-eight hundred kilometers) away.[10] Still other humpbacks travel from the coastal waters of South America and Africa. They travel at a slow, relaxed pace, about 2 to 3 miles (3 to 5 kilometers) per hour.[11]

The pregnant females arrive in Antarctica first. There is not much food for them on their trip, and they need to start eating. They have to nourish themselves and the baby whale growing inside. Next come the adolescents, which are followed by the adult male humpbacks and the females without young. Finally, the mother whales, or cows, and their young, known as calves, arrive.

All spring and summer the humpbacks fatten themselves on krill. Then, when autumn arrives and the days grow shorter, they head back to their winter grounds. By that time, their blubber has grown and become very thick. The whales will need that blubber for energy on their long return

Ocean Alliance - WHALE GALLERY - Microsoft Internet Explorer

File   Edit   View   Favorites   Tools   Help

Address http://www.oceanalliance.org/whalegallery/wg_humpback_calf_uw.html   Go

Photo: Iain Kerr

Humpback Whale - *Megaptera novaeangliae*

This photo of a humpback and her calf is from the Web site of the **Ocean Alliance,** an organization committed to the conservation of whales and their habitat.

trip and at their winter grounds, where they will have no food.

When the whales leave Antarctica, the order is reversed. Cows and calves depart first, and pregnant females leave last. They get the last gulps of krill before making the long return trip. Back near Australia, Fiji, South America, and Africa, fall and winter are much warmer than in the Southern Ocean near Antarctica.

Humpback Populations and Their Migrations

Researchers believe there are four populations of humpbacks. One is in the North Pacific, another is in the North Atlantic, a third is in the South Atlantic, and a fourth is in the Indian Ocean. The whales in one population never travel, feed, or mate with the whales in another.

The humpback whales that migrate between Australia and Antarctica are part of the group that stays in the Southern Hemisphere. Other southern humpbacks travel in the South Atlantic and Indian oceans.

North Pacific humpbacks spend spring and summer fattening themselves along the Pacific coast of the United States, from California to Alaska, as well as the Pacific coasts of Canada and Russia. Before winter sets in, they migrate to the warmer waters of Mexico, Hawaii, Costa Rica, and

Japan. North Atlantic humpbacks range from New England east to Norway in the warmer months. In the winter they migrate to the West Indies in the Caribbean Sea.

There is one population that seems to stay in the same place all year. The humpbacks that live in the Arabian Sea and northern Indian Ocean find enough food in the region all year long, and the water is warm and calm enough in winter for them to have their young.

Humpbacks migrate farther than other whales. One of the longest whale migrations ever tracked was by two humpbacks that swam from Antarctica to Isla Gorgona, Colombia, north of the equator.

This Canadian government site provides an overview of humpback whales. Information on their biology, distribution, habitat, and threats to their survival is included.

Access this Web site from http://www.myreportlinks.com

That is about fifty-eight hundred miles (ninety-three hundred kilometers)![12]

Researchers are not sure how whales manage to stay on the right course while swimming thousands of miles between their summer and winter grounds, but calves learn their migratory paths from their mothers. Some whale experts believe that whales are sensitive to the earth's magnetic field, which guides them on their migration.

How might this happen? The earth is like a giant magnet. Its magnetic force comes from its center, thousands of miles below the surface. Like other magnets, the earth has two magnetic poles, one on each end. They are the North Pole and the South Pole. Between the two poles are invisible lines of magnetic force that run from one pole to the other. These lines make up the earth's magnetic field, which may give the whales a kind of map that they can follow.[13]

Humphrey the Lost Humpback

Sometimes, a whale strays off course during its migration. The most famous whale to lose its way was a humpback that some enthusiastic whale watchers named Humphrey. This whale managed to lose his way twice.

The first time was in the fall of 1985. Humphrey was part of a breeding group of whales that live off the California coast. When he got close to San Francisco, he made his mistake. Instead of swimming around the famous Golden Gate Bridge, he went right under it. This 40-foot (13-meter) whale headed inland and spent three weeks near the mouth of the Sacramento River. Scientists in the region were worried about Humphrey because he was in freshwater, which can eventually kill a marine mammal. To guide Humphrey back to sea, a group of rescuers in a number of boats followed him. They banged on steel pipes because they knew he would not like the noise. In front of him, near the open ocean, other rescuers made what, for Humphrey, were more pleasing noises to lure him back out to sea: They broadcast the sounds of whales feeding noisily. The technique worked, and Humphrey swam out toward the Pacific Ocean.

But five years later, Humphrey was back. This time, he got himself stuck in muddy, shallow water in San Francisco Bay. The Coast Guard pulled the whale into deeper water with a huge net. Then his rescuers used the same mix of awful and pleasant noises to guide him out of the bay and back to the open ocean.[14]

Why Whales Migrate

Scientists are not sure why humpbacks and most other baleen whales leave their summer grounds to make the long journey to warmer water. The

▲ *This mother and calf swim the protected waters of the Hawaiian Islands Humpback Whale National Marine Sanctuary.*

whales use a lot of energy on these trips, partly because of their enormous size. They may migrate to avoid the fierce winter storms of the regions where they spent spring and summer. The warmer waters of their winter grounds are much calmer. That is when whales give birth to their young, and calmer waters are better for newborn whales. It would be very difficult for them to learn to blow and breathe in air during a violent winter storm like the ones that rage in Antarctica.[15]

▶ Adult Humpbacks and Their Young

Humpback mating has never been witnessed in the wild, but researchers think that female humpbacks choose a mate at their winter grounds. The whales seem to have an unusual way of pairing up. The males gather in groups to sing, but they also fight with one another, butting heads and hitting each other with their flippers.[16] The female chooses a mate from one of these groups, but researchers are not sure if the competition among males has anything to do with her choice. Some males seem to pair off with a number of females.[17]

The fetus takes a full year to develop and is usually born the following winter. No twin births have been witnessed, but that does not mean that humpbacks cannot have twins. At birth, a baby humpback weighs about fifteen hundred pounds (seven hundred kilograms) and is about sixteen feet (five meters) long. The calf soon begins to feed on its mother's rich milk. During the first few days, it may drink about ninety pounds (forty kilograms) of milk each day. All of that milk helps the calf gain weight quickly. It can gain as much as two pounds (one kilogram) in an hour![18]

For the next five or six months, the mother humpback and her young are strongly bonded to one another. The calf is always within reach of its mother. It swims right behind the small dorsal fin on her back, beneath one of her long flippers, or

Migration of the Southern Humpback Whales - Microsoft Internet Explorer

File Edit View Favorites Tools Help

Address http://www.oceania.org.au/whales/education/migration/page7.html

7   Mothers with Calves

(Photo: Trish Franklin)

The first to leave Antarctica are the females who are at the end of lactation and weaning their young. By the time they reach the mating and birthing grounds in the Great Barrier Reef, the calves have reached the yearling stage and are a little more able to look after themselves, although most

The Oceania Project organizes annual expeditions to study the whales off Australia's coast, like this mother and calf. The group's Web site includes information on expeditions, Cetacean research, and journal articles.

right alongside her. The cow may use her flipper to stroke her calf underneath its belly, or roll it playfully off her upper jaw. If an aggressive animal such as a shark threatens the young humpback, its mother will protect it.

The young whale becomes a little more independent after it arrives with its mother at their summer feeding grounds. It joins a group of young and adult humpbacks while its mother feeds. The calf continues to enjoy its mother's milk for a few more months. After it makes the return trip with its mother to their winter feeding grounds, it is ready to live independently. By then the humpback calf will be about twenty-five feet (eight meters) long.

The calf will continue to grow until it is between six and ten years old. It can begin mating before that, when it is between four and seven years of age. A humpback lives an average of fifty to sixty years. There are many dangers that may cut its life short, however. Killer whales, which are actually dolphins, and sharks attack humpbacks. But it is human activity that poses the greatest danger to humpbacks, so it is up to humans to eliminate those dangers if humpbacks are going to survive.

HOW HUMANS HAVE HARMED WHALES

Modern whales have been around for more than 3 million years.[1] For most of that time, they swam freely in the oceans, which cover 70 percent of the surface of the earth. When modern humans arrived, about one hundred thousand years ago, they did not share the earth peacefully with their great marine mammal neighbors. Humans have hunted and killed millions of whales. In more recent history, people have often harmed whales without meaning to. They have done this by striking them with ships, entangling them in fishing nets, and polluting their habitat, the oceans, with chemicals and other waste.

▶ Whaling for Survival and Profit

The indigenous, or native, peoples of the Arctic live in icy lands covered with snow much of the year. To survive in their harsh environment, these cultures have hunted whales and other marine mammals, including seals, for thousands of years. The Inuit, Yupik, Saami, and Inupiat are four of the largest native groups that still hunt. They use

▲ In this photograph from 1915, Wilson Parker, a Makah whaler, carrying sealskin floats and a harpoon, prepares to hunt. Native peoples have long depended upon whales for many of their basic needs.

the whales for their most basic needs: whale meat for food, oil for lighting, and baleen, often called whalebone, for making sleds and spears. In the summer, they use the whalebone to make frames for their skin-covered homes. Despite the moratorium on whaling, these aboriginal people have been allowed to continue subsistence whaling, on a much smaller scale—hunting certain types of whales so the aboriginal way of life can continue.

But others hunted whales for profit. European whalers began killing whales in the 1100s. By the 1600s, they had found many uses for whale parts, with whale oil for lighting being one of the most important, since electricity for lighting had not yet been discovered. By the 1700s, whale parts, such as baleen, were being used for things that would not exactly be considered necessities of life, like corsets. A whale's baleen is very springy and was perfect material for the undergarment worn by

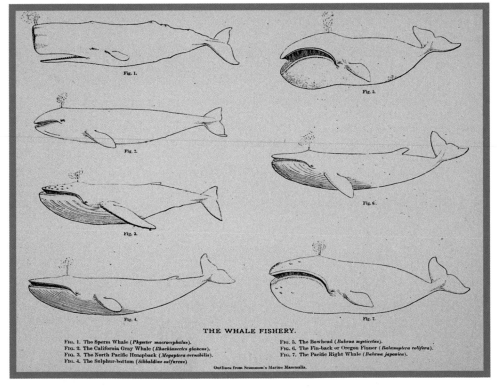

THE WHALE FISHERY.

FIG. 1. The Sperm Whale (*Physeter macrocephalus*).
FIG. 2. The California Gray Whale (*Rhachianectes glaucus*).
FIG. 3. The North Pacific Humpback (*Megaptera versabilis*).
FIG. 4. The Sulphur-bottom (*Sibbaldius sulfurens*)

FIG. 5. The Bowhead (*Balæna mysticetus*).
FIG. 6. The Fin-back or Oregon Finner (*Balænoptera velifera*).
FIG. 7. The Pacific Right Whale (*Balæna japonica*).

Outlines from Scammon's Marine Mammalia.

▲ In "The Whale Fishery," a historic drawing, the humpback whale is pictured as the third whale in the left-hand column.

women. A corset was pulled around the waist and laced tightly to make women look slender. Baleen was also used to make umbrellas and even clocks.

Whaling in America

In the 1700s, American colonists began hunting right whales off the New England and mid-Atlantic coasts. These baleen whales were named right whales because whalers considered them the "right" whales to hunt, since they were rich in blubber and relatively easy to catch. Then, in 1712, a crew of sailors from Nantucket island, in the Massachusetts Bay Colony, killed a sperm whale and melted its blubber into whale oil.[2] They discovered that it was better than other whale oil. The sperm whale provided two other precious products. Ambergris, from the animal's intestine, could be used to make perfume. Spermaceti, from the whale's head, was a fine oil that burned with no smell or smoke.

By the late 1700s, American whalers were chasing sperm whales as far south as Brazil, in South America, and as far north as Newfoundland, Canada. Over the next century, migrating North Atlantic humpbacks became targets, too.

Whaling reached its peak in America in the mid-1800s. The beautiful homes of wealthy whaling captains lined the streets of Nantucket and other New England ports. By then, whale boats were built for long trips and large crews. One whaling boat carried eight lightweight smaller boats and a crew of up to fifty men. Some boats left port for years at a time.

▷ Whaling New England Style: The "Nantucket Sleigh Ride"

When the New England whalers spotted a whale from their large boat, they got into smaller boats to chase it. One man aboard each small boat would throw a harpoon, which was like a spear with a fishhook at one end and a strong rope tied to the other end. The rope was attached to the boat. Sometimes the whale became angry and dragged the small boat with the harpooner on a

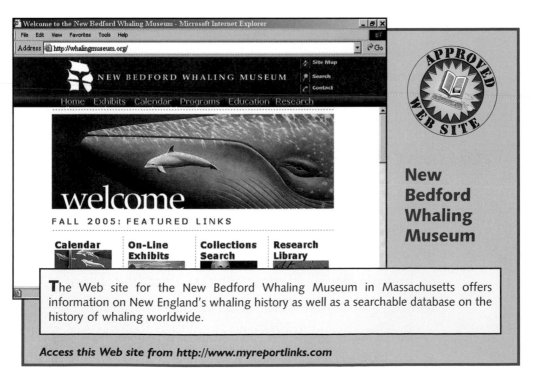

The Web site for the New Bedford Whaling Museum in Massachusetts offers information on New England's whaling history as well as a searchable database on the history of whaling worldwide.

Access this Web site from http://www.myreportlinks.com

wild ride. Whalers called it the Nantucket sleigh ride. It was the beginning of a horrible death for the whale. After the whale exhausted itself, someone killed it with a spear. Then the men cut up the whale and hauled it on board the large boat. The blubber was melted right there in big iron pots. This crude method of killing whales is still used in some poor island communities.

Modern Whaling

Modern commercial whaling began with the invention of the exploding harpoon in 1864.[3] A harpooner fired a harpoon with a grenade on its tip from a cannon in the front of a boat. The harpoon went inside the whale's body and exploded. Similar harpoons are used in whaling today. The use of compressed air to inflate the carcasses of rorquals was another feature of modern whaling. The air kept the whale from sinking after it was killed.

Around the same time that the exploding harpoon was invented, steam-powered boats began to replace sailboats. The steamboats were larger and faster and could go all the way to Antarctica, where whalers had never been before. Thousands of humpbacks and other whales that had been feeding safely near Antarctica were in danger.

By the 1920s, the first factory ships headed for Antarctica and remained there the entire spring and summer feeding season. These industrial ships collected and processed whales on a large scale. The whales were killed by exploding harpoons fired from smaller catcher boats. Whalers on the catcher boats then brought the whale carcasses to the factory ships, where workers butchered the whales and froze the meat.

As whalers became more efficient, the populations of the largest whales, including humpbacks, shrank dramatically. More than 2 million of the larger whales were killed in the Southern Hemisphere alone in the twentieth century.[4] Whale populations in other parts of the world were slaughtered, too. In Hawaii, whalers killed

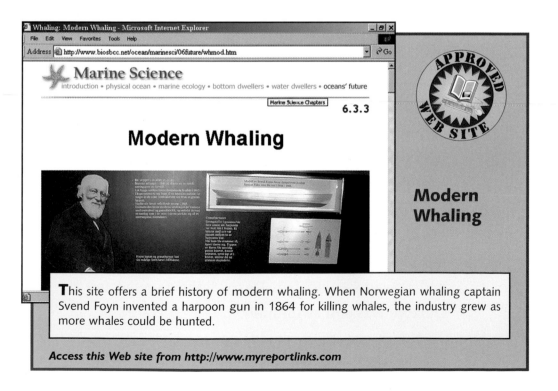

This site offers a brief history of modern whaling. When Norwegian whaling captain Svend Foyn invented a harpoon gun in 1864 for killing whales, the industry grew as more whales could be hunted.

Access this Web site from http://www.myreportlinks.com

humbacks during stopovers in the islands for provisions on their journeys to the South Pacific to kill sperm whales. Between 1905 and 1965, the Northern Pacific humpback population dropped from about fifteen thousand to one thousand.[5]

Today, most countries have stopped whaling for profit. The native people of some of the world's island communities kill one or two humpbacks each year for basic needs such as food. Among these islanders are residents of St. Vincent and the Grenadines, in the Caribbean Sea.

Fishing Equipment Can Be Dangerous to Whales

Early one morning in 1990, some researchers were cruising in the southern Gulf of Maine, off the coast of New England. They spotted a female humpback whale they knew well named Quixote, who was entangled in more than 100 yards (91 meters) of fishing net. The researchers thought that she had swum into the net while chasing fish near the ocean bottom. They guessed that she had rolled to try to get out of the net, which had just made things worse. The net, which was coming out of both sides of her mouth, crossed her back and trailed behind her. Despite the tangled net, Quixote was still swimming.

No rescue team could arrive that day. The researchers lost track of Quixote and were afraid

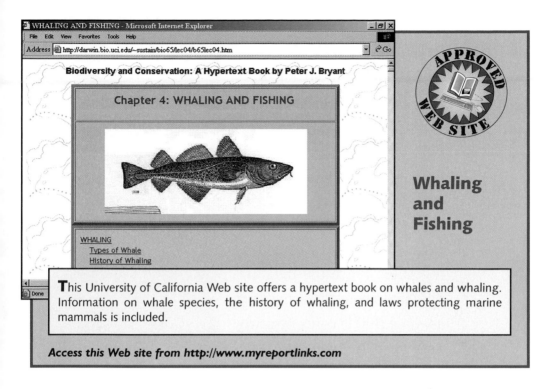

WHALING AND FISHING - Microsoft Internet Explorer

File Edit View Favorites Tools Help

Address http://darwin.bio.uci.edu/~sustain/bio65/lec04/b65lec04.htm

Biodiversity and Conservation: A Hypertext Book by Peter J. Bryant

Chapter 4: WHALING AND FISHING

WHALING
Types of Whale
History of Whaling

Whaling and Fishing

This University of California Web site offers a hypertext book on whales and whaling. Information on whale species, the history of whaling, and laws protecting marine mammals is included.

Access this Web site from http://www.myreportlinks.com

she had died. But several months later, she was seen again. Somehow, Quixote had managed to disentangle herself.

About 70 percent of the humpback whales that feed in New England's waters have become entangled in nets or other types of fishing gear at some point in their lives.[6] The net in which Quixote had become entangled was a gill net. Gill nets, used by fishermen around the world, are made of a fine mesh that catches fish by entangling their gills. In the northeastern United States, fishermen set out gill nets and leave them overnight. When they haul the nets in the next day, they hope to find cod, haddock, or dogfish caught in the net, but they certainly do not hope to find a whale.

Gill nets are strong nets that sit upright in the water like a series of giant tennis nets. Each one can be as high as 10 feet (3 meters) and as long as 300 feet (91 meters). Fishermen sometimes put ten of these nets together.[7] Since the nets are difficult to detect, it is easy for a whale that is concentrating on doing its own fishing to swim right into one.

Until recently, fishermen around the world also used drift nets. They hung these nets from buoys and let them drift in the water. Many of the nets were enormous. Some stretched between 30 and 50 miles (48 and 80 kilometers).[8] Hundreds of

Lobster traps, like the ones pictured, are often strung together with traplines, which sometimes entangle whales.

thousands of marine mammals have died in these invisible nylon nets. Many seabirds and sea turtles have been killed by them as well. In 1991, the United Nations called for an end to drift netting on the high seas. More recently the European Union, an economic and political organization of European governments, banned the use of drift nets in most of the waters of its member nations.

▶ Trapping More Than Lobsters

In New England, humpbacks become entangled in lobster traps as well as nets. The idea of a whale caught in a lobster trap sounds ridiculous. After all, a lobster trap is only a few feet long, and a humpback is more than forty feet long. The whale does not get caught in the trap itself—at least, not at first. Lobstermen string together a series of their traps with strong lines called traplines, which can be up to 100 feet (30 meters) long. Traplines float in the water in the shape of an arch that can be up to 30 feet (9 meters) high. The whale becomes entangled in the line, and the trap may end up on some part of its body, worsening the problem. In other regions of the United States, similar gear is used to catch crabs. Humpbacks, other whales, and many other marine mammals and seabirds also become trapped—and sometimes killed— by longlines, which are fishing lines that have many baited hooks.

Chemical Pollution in the Ocean

In the last century, chemists working in different industries have created many types of synthetic chemicals—chemicals that do not occur in nature. Some synthetic chemicals enter rivers and streams directly from factories and flow into the ocean. Others enter the ocean as runoff. For example, when an agricultural company sprays a large crop of corn with chemicals to get rid of destructive insects, some of these chemicals are washed off when it rains. They can end up in streams, rivers, and eventually the ocean.

Synthetic chemicals do not break down as quickly as natural ones. When they end up in the ocean, they can remain there a long time. Some of these chemicals do not dissolve in water. But they will dissolve in the fatty tissue of a tiny fish or a large whale. Some of the most polluting chemicals in the ocean are polychlorinated biphenyls, or PCBs. These compounds were once used in a wide variety of products, from electrical equipment to paints, but they were found to be a very toxic pollutant. PCBs tend to accumulate in the tissues of animals and become more concentrated the higher up in the food chain the animal is. When a whale eats fish with PCBs in their tissue, the whale will eventually have a very high concentration of PCBs in its own tissue. The PCBs can disrupt the way the whale's body is supposed to function. If a

▲ Humpback whales are not the only marine mammals to be exposed to dangerous toxins. Killer whales, like this one pictured spyhopping, have also been found to contain dangerous levels of PCBs in their blubber.

mother whale has a lot of PCBs or other toxic chemicals in her body, she passes it along to her calf when it nurses.

In 1977, Congress passed a law that made it illegal to manufacture PCBs. But a great amount of damage had already been done. By then, American companies had manufactured more than 1.5 billion pounds (680 million kilograms) of PCBs.[9] High levels of PCBs and similar chemicals have been found in the blubber of many marine mammals, including beluga whales and killer whales.

Noise Pollution in the Ocean

A noise cannot really poison ocean water. But loud sounds may make it difficult for whales to communicate with one another over long distances. They may also make it difficult for whales to hear important noises, such as the approach of a group of dangerous killer whales.

Loud sounds in the ocean environment come from a number of sources. The very large boats traveling the world's oceans, such as giant oil tankers, are one source. Even a lot of whale-watching boats traveling in and out of a small humpback feeding area may be too noisy. When petroleum companies explore the ocean to look for new sources of oil and gas, they sometimes intentionally set off small explosions. The United States military creates noise pollution, too. In order to find an enemy's submarine in the ocean, it uses sonar, a method or device that can detect an object in the ocean and discover its location through sound waves. It does this by creating very loud sounds, which echo in the water and are reflected by objects.

In the ocean, sounds travel much farther and faster than they do in the air. Sounds produced by sonar can travel for hundreds of miles.[10] These loud noises may stop whales from feeding. They can also affect a whale permanently. If a whale is too close, the sound can injure its hearing and can cause bleeding in its brain, which will kill it. Pressured by environmental groups, the United States Navy has limited its use of sonar during peacetime, although not enough, according to some conservationists.

Collisions With Ships

Large ships also pose a danger to humpbacks and other whales. Between 20 and 35 percent of the whales that are found dead were probably accidentally hit by a ship.[11] As oceangoing ships have become larger and faster, the number of these collisions has grown. As whales mature, some of them, including humpbacks, seem to learn how to avoid ships. Many of the humpbacks that collide with ships are young. If a boat hits a whale and the whale is injured, it sometimes has difficulty

This right whale was killed when it collided with a ship and was cut by the propeller. At the NOAA Web site for **National Marine Sanctuaries,** learn more about threats to whales posed by humans and human-led activity.

swimming and becomes stranded on a beach. If it is lucky and its injuries are not too severe, rescuers may be able to find it and help it back into the water.

▶ Global Warming

Most scientists believe that a great change is taking place in every climate around the world. They believe that the average temperature on earth is rising as a result of human activities. The change is called global warming.

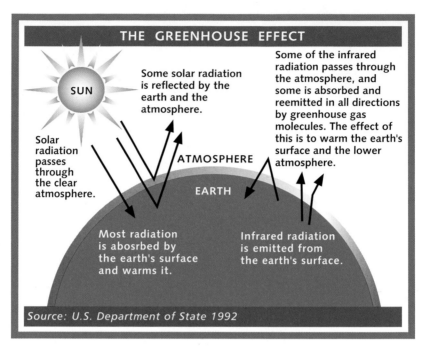

THE GREENHOUSE EFFECT

SUN

Some solar radiation is reflected by the earth and the atmosphere.

Some of the infrared radiation passes through the atmosphere, and some is absorbed and reemitted in all directions by greenhouse gas molecules. The effect of this is to warm the earth's surface and the lower atmosphere.

Solar radiation passes through the clear atmosphere.

ATMOSPHERE

EARTH

Most radiation is abosrbed by the earth's surface and warms it.

Infrared radiation is emitted from the earth's surface.

Source: U.S. Department of State 1992

▲ Global warming may have a huge impact on whether whales and other marine animals survive long into the future. This diagram explains the greenhouse effect, which plays a large part in why the earth and its waters are heating up.

Global warming has to do with the earth's ability to bounce much of the radiation that it receives from the sun back into space. Many activities in the modern world, from manufacturing to driving automobiles, pollute the atmosphere with carbon dioxide, water vapor, methane, and other gases known as greenhouse gases. They are called greenhouse gases because they trap heat in the earth's atmosphere rather than allowing it to be reflected back into space. Many scientists think that a buildup of these gases is causing the earth's atmosphere to absorb more of the sun's radiation and bounce less of it back into space.

Global warming is also affecting ocean environments, which seem to be changing more quickly now than they ever have since modern marine mammals have been in existence. Dramatic changes are taking place near the North Pole and the South Pole. One important event occurred on the coast of Ellesmere Island, which lies in the Arctic Ocean in northern Canada. An ice shelf has been there for at least three thousand years. In the summer of 2003, it cracked and some large islands of ice drifted away.

Many scientists believe the ice shelf cracked because the Arctic Ocean is warming. Even more

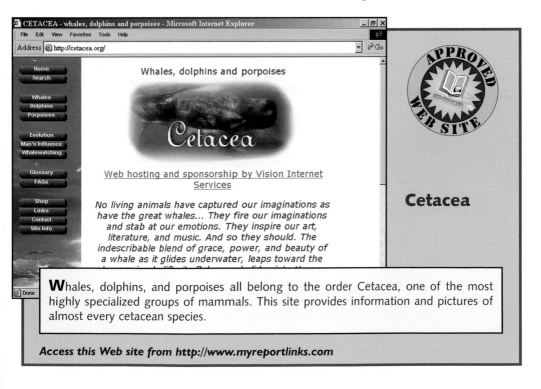

Whales, dolphins, and porpoises all belong to the order Cetacea, one of the most highly specialized groups of mammals. This site provides information and pictures of almost every cetacean species.

Access this Web site from http://www.myreportlinks.com

dramatic changes are taking place in Antarctica. Just a year before the Ellesmere Island ice shelf cracked, a much larger one shattered into thousands of icebergs in Antarctica.[12] The radiation from the sun that is warming the oceans in the poles may destroy the tiny plants that are part of the ocean's chain of life. If the krill in Antarctica have no plants to eat, they may die out in those regions. Since they are a very important source of food for humpbacks and other animals, those animals will suffer.

▶ Global Concern

People worldwide are concerned about global warming. The governments of more than 120 countries have signed a document called the Kyoto Protocol. They have agreed to greatly reduce the level of harmful gases that they release into the atmosphere. So far the United States has not signed this agreement. It claims that the adjustments that would have to be made in the nation's power plants and in some industries would harm its economy.

Although the United States has failed to sign the Kyoto Protocol, it has passed some important laws to protect humpback whales and other endangered animals. It also participates in meetings of the International Whaling Commission.

Chapter 4 ▶

THE STRUGGLE TO SAVE HUMPBACKS AND OTHER WHALES

On June 27, 1975, a Russian whaling boat was chasing sperm whales in the Pacific Ocean. Mounted on the front of the boat was a cannon loaded with an exploding harpoon. The whales were exhausted, and the harpooner was getting ready to kill one of them. Behind the whaling boat was the factory boat, waiting to process the freshly killed carcass. For the harpooner, it would have

Greenpeace International is a conservation organization dedicated to saving the fragile ecosystems of the earth. At its Web site, learn more about this group and its work to save whales and other species.

Access this Web site from http://www.myreportlinks.com

been a typical day hunting whales if it were not for some strange boats in the water.

Six men in three small inflatable boats had put themselves between the harpooner and the whales. They were from a conservation organization called Greenpeace, founded in Canada in 1971. These men were trying to protect the whales by placing themselves in front of the harpooner. You might call them extreme conservationists. They were guessing that the harpooner would rather let the whales go free than risk harming a human being. But they were wrong.

The harpooner fired his harpoon. It shot right over the heads of two men in one of the inflatable boats and hit the back of a whale. The ocean suddenly erupted in an explosion of sea spray and blood. Fortunately, the men in the inflatable boats were not hurt. The whale was not as lucky.

▷ The World Watches

Although the Greenpeace activists did not manage to save the sperm whale that day, they helped save thousands of whales indirectly. One of them had a movie camera, and he managed to record the whole bloody event. Greenpeace sent the film to television news stations around the world. Many people who had never thought much about whales were now horrified to see a sperm whale die while they watched the evening news. Some of those people decided then that it was important to help save whales.[1]

Saving the Whales

Greenpeace was part of a growing international conservation movement. People were becoming concerned that all the new development around the world was injuring the great web of wild plants and animals on the earth. They were afraid that too many of them would disappear as power plants multiplied, cars filled the highways, and trees from ancient forests were cut down for lumber.

When National Geographic's recording of humpback whale songs was released in 1970, it created a lot of sympathy for whales. An increasing number of people thought that humpbacks and other whales should not be slaughtered for their meat or oil. "Save the whales" became a slogan of the conservation movement.

By 1970, the United States had already passed several important laws that helped protect whales and other wildlife. In 1966, Congress passed the Endangered Species Preservation Act, which listed native species that were threatened with extinction, but it offered limited protection. Three years later, a stronger bill, the Endangered Species Conservation Act of 1969, improved upon the earlier act. It provided protection to species that were in danger of becoming extinct worldwide.

Under the act, the humpback whale was first listed as an endangered species in June 1970.

In 1972, Congress passed the Marine Mammal Protection Act (MMPA). The MMPA made it illegal for an American citizen to kill a whale or import whale products into the country.

That same year, Congress passed the Marine Protection, Research and Sanctuaries Act of 1972. The law focused on improving the health of the oceans. It also promised extra protection for important regions within the nation's coastal waters that should be conserved.

The Endangered Species Act of 1973

The next year, 1973, Congress passed the Endangered Species Act. That law made it illegal to kill, injure, or capture any animal species that was in danger of becoming extinct, or disappearing from the earth. The United States government consulted many scientists when it prepared its list of endangered species. Eight whales were listed, including the humpback. It will remain on the endangered list until the government and scientists agree that it is no longer in danger of becoming extinct.

The Marine Mammal Protection Act and the Endangered Species Act were United States laws that helped protect humpbacks and other endangered whales. But those two laws were not enough to save humpbacks and other whales from the harpooners and factory boats that sailed from Japan, Russia, Norway, and other nations around the world. The organization that had the most power to save the whales was the International Whaling Commission (IWC).

The International Whaling Commission

The IWC was established in 1948. All of its member nations had whaling industries, including the United States. Representatives of these nations came together once a year to decide on a quota, the maximum number of whales that could be killed in the next whaling season. They agreed

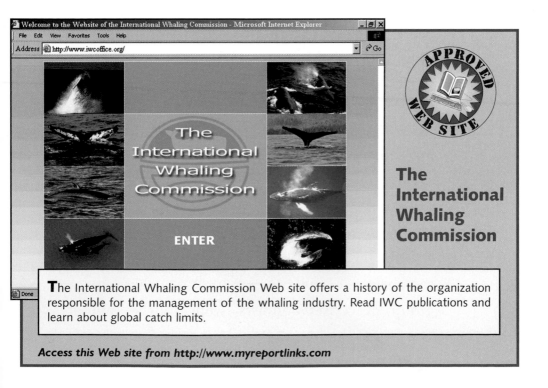

The International Whaling Commission Web site offers a history of the organization responsible for the management of the whaling industry. Read IWC publications and learn about global catch limits.

Access this Web site from http://www.myreportlinks.com

that when they reached the quota, they would stop whaling for the year. The members of the IWC set their quotas so that they would not destroy the whale populations. The whaling nations wanted to make sure there would always be enough whales in the ocean for them to hunt.

But the quota system has not worked well. IWC members did not consult any scientists to set their quota. They came up with a number that seemed right to them. Some member nations ignored the quota. At least one country, the Soviet Union, was not truthful about how many whales it was killing. Between World War II and 1972, the Russians and other members of what was then the Soviet Union killed 48,477 humpbacks. During all of those years, they reported that they had killed a total of only 2,700 whales.[2]

Conservationists Fight the IWC

In 1972, the United Nations took a stand to protect whales. At a meeting about the environment, the representatives of all fifty-two nations who were at the meeting voted in favor of a ten-year moratorium on commercial whaling.[3] That meant that for ten years, there would be no whaling for the purpose of making money. Two weeks later, a group of conservationists went to the annual meeting of the International Whaling Commission and urged the IWC to vote on the United Nation's

The American Cetacean Society, founded in 1967, is the oldest whale conservation association in the world. Learn more about its work, which includes research on marine mammals, the survivability of species, and habitat protection.

Access this Web site from http://www.myreportlinks.com

proposal for a moratorium on whaling. In the vote that followed, the United States, Britain, Argentina, and Mexico voted in favor of the moratorium. However, Japan, Russia, Norway, Iceland, South Africa, and Panama voted against it and soundly defeated the proposal. (Four countries, France, Denmark, Canada, and Australia, did not vote at all.) In the end, the IWC controlled the fate of the whales, not the United Nations. The pro-whaling nations went right on hunting whales.

A Historic Vote for Whales

Until the late 1970s, the International Whaling Commission remained an organization of fewer

▲ In this photo from the 1940s, humpbacks killed by whalers have been inflated with compressed air and are floating bottom side up, waiting to be hauled onto a factory ship and butchered.

than twenty nations. Then in 1979, along came the Seychelles, a group of islands off the east coast of Africa. This nation of only sixty-four thousand people joined the IWC and managed to turn it upside down. The Seychelles was very much against whaling. Its representative to the IWC was a man named Lyall Watson. With the help of Greenpeace and other conservation organizations, Watson convinced more antiwhaling nations to join the IWC.

By 1982, there were thirty-seven member nations in the IWC. That year, when the delegates began gathering for the annual meeting, the conservationists thought they would have enough votes to pass a moratorium on whaling.

The meeting was in a hotel in Brighton, on England's south coast. Two Greenpeace ships were outside on the water, waiting silently for the IWC's vote. A group of antiwhaling people waited outside, too. When the vote for a moratorium was taken, twenty-five countries voted in favor of the moratorium and seven voted against it. The moratorium finally passed!

People inside the hotel and outside jumped up and down and cheered. A van drove by, blasting whale songs from its speakers. A freshly made banner on the van read "Whales Saved—Brighton 1982."[4]

Thousands of Whales Saved, But Not All

The whaling moratorium, which was supposed to be temporary, is still in effect today. Its purpose was to give IWC members a chance to study the health and size of the whale populations. There are ways to get around the moratorium, however. Countries can get permission from the IWC to kill whales for scientific purposes. Then they can sell the whale meat. Japan has killed seven hundred whales each year through permits granted for scientific study. Recently, Iceland began following Japan's example.

Even though it has not stopped all whaling, the IWC's moratorium has done more to save whales than any other action taken by an organization or a government. Roger Payne commented, "Were it not for the IWC there would probably be no right, bowhead, gray or blue whales left in the world, and humpbacks . . . would probably be extinct in the Southern Hemisphere."[5]

Many humpback populations seem to be on the road to recovery. When the moratorium went into effect, there were about fifteen thousand humpbacks.[6] Researchers estimate that there are now between twenty-five thousand and thirty thousand.[7]

National Marine Sanctuaries

To help whales recover from centuries of whale hunting, the United States has established two sanctuaries in ocean regions that are important whale habitats: one in New England and one in Hawaii. These two marine sanctuaries and eleven others were established as a result of the Marine Protection, Research and Sanctuaries Act of 1972.

The warm waters of the Hawaiian Islands Humpback Whale National Marine Sanctuary are the winter grounds for about two thirds of the North Pacific humpback whale population. According to scientists, this sanctuary is one of the most important habitats for humpbacks in the world. The whales come here to mate, give birth to their young, and most likely to escape the winter storms to the north.

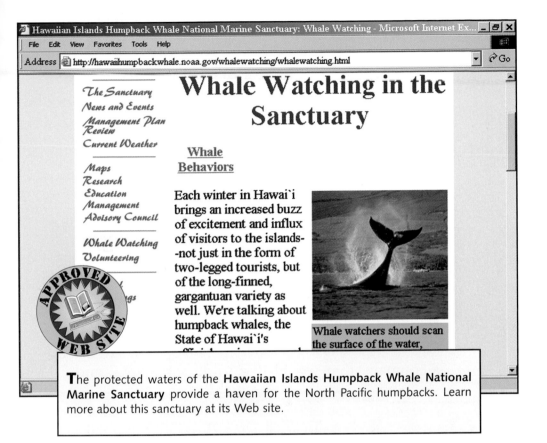

Hawaiian Islands Humpback Whale National Marine Sanctuary: Whale Watching - Microsoft Internet Ex...

File   Edit   View   Favorites   Tools   Help

Address 🔲 http://hawaiihumpbackwhale.noaa.gov/whalewatching/whalewatching.html   ▼ 🔗 Go

The Sanctuary
News and Events
Management Plan Review
Current Weather

Maps
Research
Education
Management Advisory Council

Whale Watching
Volunteering

Whale Watching in the Sanctuary

Whale Behaviors

Each winter in Hawai`i brings an increased buzz of excitement and influx of visitors to the islands--not just in the form of two-legged tourists, but of the long-finned, gargantuan variety as well. We're talking about humpback whales, the State of Hawai`i's

Whale watchers should scan the surface of the water,

The protected waters of the **Hawaiian Islands Humpback Whale National Marine Sanctuary** provide a haven for the North Pacific humpbacks. Learn more about this sanctuary at its Web site.

Unlike the Hawaiian sanctuary, the Gerry E. Studds-Stellwagen Bank National Marine Sanctuary, about twenty-six miles (forty-two kilometers) east of Boston, is a feeding ground, not a mating ground. In spring and summer, humpbacks and fin whales feed among its 842 square miles (2,180 square kilometers) of shallow waters. Stellwagen Bank draws many researchers to observe the whale populations that feed in its waters, but researchers are not the only ones to visit the sanctuary. About a million people take whale-watching cruises there. The World Wildlife Fund has called it one of the ten best whale-watching places in the world.[8]

Conservationists would like these sanctuaries to be like nature preserves—they want the whales to be able to enjoy an environment that is as free from human disturbance as possible. But when the staff of a sanctuary creates a plan for what human activities can go on there, they have to balance the needs of the whales with the needs of the people who work within the sanctuary. At Stellwagen Bank, fishermen continue to fish in the sanctuary's waters, and there is even a shipping lane that goes right through the middle of it. On the other hand, a company that would like to do some sand and

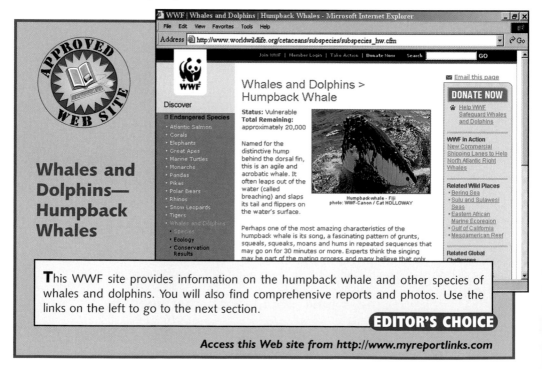

Whales and Dolphins— Humpback Whales

This WWF site provides information on the humpback whale and other species of whales and dolphins. You will also find comprehensive reports and photos. Use the links on the left to go to the next section.

EDITOR'S CHOICE

Access this Web site from http://www.myreportlinks.com

gravel mining at Stellwagen would not be allowed to do so because that would greatly disturb the whales' habitat.

There are other marine sanctuaries in the world. The Ligurian Sea Cetacean Sanctuary in the western Mediterranean Sea is a feeding ground for fin whales. Member nations of the European Union are planning to establish marine sanctuaries for dolphins and porpoises near the shores of the Mediterranean.

The IUCN's Red List

For the last four decades, an international organization known as the IUCN-World Conservation Union has been keeping track of plant and animal species around the world. When a plant or animal is in danger of becoming extinct or needs extra protection, the IUCN puts it on the organization's Red List. The purpose of the list is to alert people around the world so that they can take some action to protect the plant or animal. There are seven categories that the IUCN uses on its Red List to describe how endangered the plant or animal is, from *extinct* to *least concern*. Humpbacks were once listed as endangered. In 1990 their status changed to *vulnerable,* which falls near the middle of these categories.

More than ten thousand experts from around the world volunteer their time to help the IUCN

▲ *Humpback whales in the waters of the Southern Ocean, the ocean surrounding Antarctica.*

with its work. Some of them belong to the Cetacean Specialist Group, which focuses on the problems of marine mammals. In 2003, this group published a new action plan for all cetaceans. The group recommended that conservationists focus on important populations within a species in addition to the species as a whole. For example, the IUCN might consider the humpbacks in the

Southern Hemisphere endangered, not vulnerable. This population suffered more than other humpbacks before all commercial whaling stopped. As a result, it will take these humpbacks longer to recover.[9]

International Agreements

Two important international agreements have also helped conserve whales. One is the Convention on the Conservation of Migratory Species of Wild Animals, usually referred to as the Convention on Migratory Species, or CMS. Under this agreement, ninety-one countries work together to protect animals that migrate, including birds and marine mammals.

The other is the Convention on International Trade in Endangered Species of Wild Flora and Fauna, or CITES. One hundred sixty-nine countries now voluntarily abide by CITES, which tries to ensure that the international trade in products made from plants and animals does not endanger their survival. CITES forbids its members from selling or buying any products made from whales.[10] These international agreements have helped humpbacks and other endangered animals to survive.

Chapter 5

WHAT SCIENTISTS AND CONSERVATIONISTS ARE DOING

One early spring weekend, a group of scientists, conservationists, and whale watchers got together for an all-day meeting. They sat around looking at photos of humpback flukes and tried to decide what the black-and-white patterns reminded them of. There was a very good reason for this strange activity. They were using the unique pattern on each set of flukes to name the seventy-five humpbacks that were new to the summer feeding grounds in New England the previous year.

Naming the whales was not easy work, however. The name could not be a human name, and it could not be masculine or feminine because the scientists often did not know whether the whale was a male or female. To make matters more difficult, it had to be a name that had not already been used for a humpback. Whale watchers and experts around Stellwagen Bank had been identifying whales for decades. A lot of the names that came to mind were already taken.

On one whale's flukes there was a mark that looked like the number fourteen. So, of course,

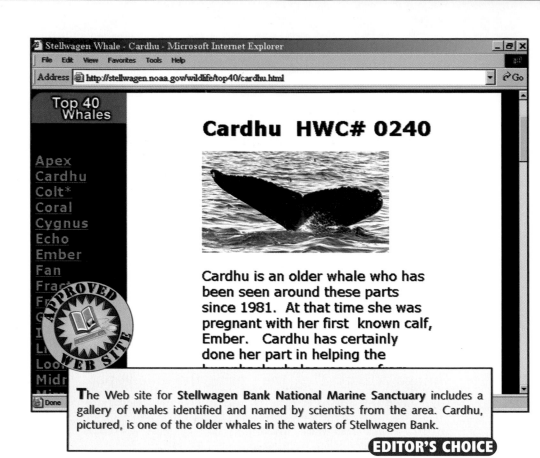

Stellwagen Whale - Cardhu - Microsoft Internet Explorer

File   Edit   View   Favorites   Tools   Help

Address http://stellwagen.noaa.gov/wildlife/top40/cardhu.html   Go

Top 40
Whales

Apex
Cardhu
Colt*
Coral
Cygnus
Echo
Ember
Fan
Frac
F
G
I
L
Loo
Midr

Cardhu HWC# 0240

Cardhu is an older whale who has
been seen around these parts
since 1981. At that time she was
pregnant with her first known calf,
Ember.   Cardhu has certainly
done her part in helping the

The Web site for **Stellwagen Bank National Marine Sanctuary** includes a
gallery of whales identified and named by scientists from the area. Cardhu,
pictured, is one of the older whales in the waters of Stellwagen Bank.

EDITOR'S CHOICE

someone wanted to name the whale "Fourteen."
Someone else thought that the Spanish word for
fourteen, which is *catorce,* sounded better. After
some debate, *Fourteen* won. The group named
another whale *Cardhu,* a Gaelic term meaning
"black rock." And they called a third one Pez
because it had a mark shaped like a Pez candy dis-
penser. The members of the group hoped they
would have a chance to see many of these whales
out on the ocean. About one thousand humpbacks
visit the region regularly.[1]

Over the years, many humpbacks have become well known to local researchers and whale watchers. One of those whales is Molson, the inventor of a feeding technique that included slamming her tail on the water. The first humpback named was Salt, a large female that was first sighted in 1976. Salt was often seen in New England waters. When someone identified her swimming in the waters off the Dominican Republic, researchers became very excited. Salt was proof that humpbacks from New England migrated to the humpbacks' winter grounds in the Caribbean Sea.[2]

▶ Identifying Whales

On most whale-watching boats that go out in New England waters, scientists or naturalists will identify individual whales for passengers. The people who observe the humpbacks in the waters of Stellwagen Bank give them names because it is fun for the naturalist on a whale-watching boat to introduce a whale by its name to the people on the boat. In the rest of New England and around the world, each whale is identified by a specific number. The whale's name and number make it easier for researchers and conservationists to exchange information about the whale and its behavior.

This exchange of information is important. Some humpbacks may come back to the same summer feeding ground year after year, but others

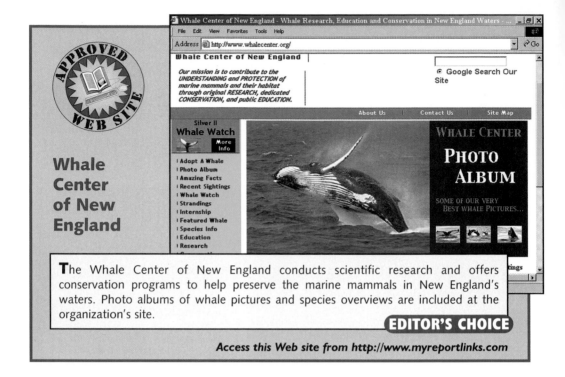

The Whale Center of New England conducts scientific research and offers conservation programs to help preserve the marine mammals in New England's waters. Photo albums of whale pictures and species overviews are included at the organization's site.

EDITOR'S CHOICE

Access this Web site from http://www.myreportlinks.com

seem to move around. The humpback named Quixote that was found entangled in fishing gear near Stellwagen Bank in 1990 came back to Stellwagen the next year. But then no one identified her again until 1997, when researchers from Stellwagen Bank learned from their colleagues that she had been sighted in the Gulf of St. Lawrence, in Canada. Researchers in the Stellwagen region were thrilled when Quixote came back with a calf two years later.

By knowing the identity of a whale and exchanging information with other scientists, researchers can keep track of a whale's age if it was first identified when it was a calf. Researchers may also be able to keep track of the number of calves that a female has had and the problems a whale has experienced throughout its life. The more information that researchers can gather about the life stories of humpbacks, the better prepared they are to help conserve humpback populations.

In order to identify a humpback, researchers look at a collection of photos of humpback flukes with the names or numbers of the whales. The Provincetown Center for Coastal Studies, on Cape Cod, Massachusetts, keeps about eighteen hundred whale photos to help researchers identify the humpbacks from Nantucket north to Nova Scotia, in Canada, and east to Georges Bank, a submerged sandbank east of Cape Cod.[3]

A photograph of the pattern on a whale's flukes is not the only way that researchers identify these whales. Over the years, a whale's flukes may become scratched or cut, and its tail may not match a photograph taken earlier.

Tissue Sampling

Scientists have another, more exact way of identifying whales. Some work with tissue samples from humpbacks. To get the sample, a researcher fires a specially designed arrow from a crossbow. When the arrow hits a whale, it bounces off, drawing a little bit of the whale's skin and blubber with it.

The distinctive markings on each humpback's flukes help researchers identify the whales.

Then the arrow floats on the water until the researcher picks it up.

Scientists can use the whale tissue to do more than simply identify the whale. They can use whale tissue to analyze the whale's genes. These are parts of the cells of every living thing. Like all plants and animals, a humpback inherits its genes from its parents. By analyzing the genes in a tissue sample, a researcher can learn about a whale's parents as well as about the whale itself. Scientists have learned through genetic analysis that there may be a greater number of separate humpback populations than they had thought. Even though some of these populations mingle with each other at their summer or winter grounds, they may not mate with one another.[4] Tissue samples can also show researchers what a whale likes to eat, how old it is, and the level of toxins in its body from pollution.

Learning More About Whales

Researchers all over the world are using tissue samples and other techniques to learn more about whale populations. Some countries are working together to study the humpbacks that migrate in their part of the world. One of the most important questions that they want to answer is whether the humpback population they are studying is increasing in number and by how much.

Years of the North Atlantic Humpbacks (YoNAH)

In the early 1990s, researchers from the United States, the Dominican Republic, Greenland, Norway, Iceland, Canada, the United Kingdom, and Denmark conducted a research project together on North Atlantic humpbacks. The project is called the Years of the North Atlantic Humpbacks, or YoNAH. For two years, researchers photographed humpback flukes and took tissue

▲ A pair of humpbacks swim in the North Atlantic.

samples in their summer and winter feeding grounds. Their summer grounds range from the New England coast northeast to the coast of Norway in the Norwegian Sea. Their winter grounds are in a smaller region of the Caribbean Sea, between the Dominican Republic and the West Indies.

The researchers estimated that there were about 10,600 North Atlantic humpbacks. It was the first precise estimate ever made of the whole North Atlantic population.[5] A second survey of the whale population was completed in 2004 and 2005. The results are now being analyzed by scientists. Eventually they will be able to calculate how much the North Atlantic humpback population has grown since the first survey.

SPLASH—A Study of North Pacific Humpbacks

A three-year international study of North Pacific humpbacks, similar to YoNAH, is now under way. The study is called the Structure of Populations, Levels of Abundance and Status of Humpbacks, or SPLASH. Scientists from the United States, Canada, and Mexico are working together to get photographs of flukes and tissue samples of the humpbacks. Hundreds of researchers are taking these photos and tissue samples in the whales' winter grounds in Hawaii, Mexico, and Central

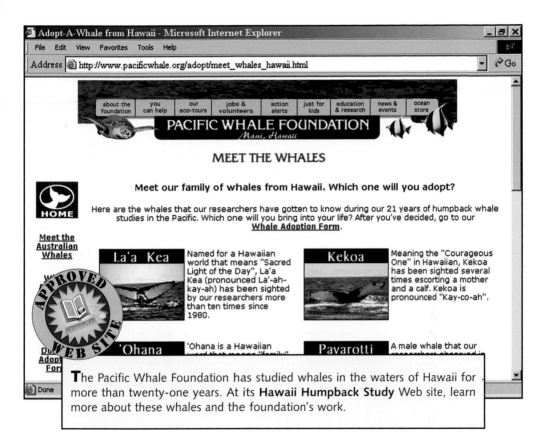

Adopt-A-Whale from Hawaii - Microsoft Internet Explorer

File   Edit   View   Favorites   Tools   Help

Address http://www.pacificwhale.org/adopt/meet_whales_hawaii.html   Go

about the foundation | you can help | our eco-tours | jobs & volunteers | action alerts | just for kids | education & research | news & events | ocean store

PACIFIC WHALE FOUNDATION
Maui, Hawaii

MEET THE WHALES

Meet our family of whales from Hawaii. Which one will you adopt?

Here are the whales that our researchers have gotten to know during our 21 years of humpback whale studies in the Pacific. Which one will you bring into your life? After you've decided, go to our **Whale Adoption Form**.

HOME

Meet the Australian Whales

La'a Kea — Named for a Hawaiian world that means "Sacred Light of the Day", La'a Kea (pronounced La'-ah-kay-ah) has been sighted by our researchers more than ten times since 1980.

Kekoa — Meaning the "Courageous One" in Hawaiian, Kekoa has been sighted several times escorting a mother and a calf. Kekoa is pronounced "Kay-co-ah".

'Ohana — 'Ohana is a Hawaiian word that means "family."

Pavarotti — A male whale that our researchers observed in

Done

The Pacific Whale Foundation has studied whales in the waters of Hawaii for more than twenty-one years. At its **Hawaii Humpback Study** Web site, learn more about these whales and the foundation's work.

America and in their summer feeding grounds to the north, including the west coast of Alaska, Canada, and the Aleutian Islands of southwestern Alaska.

Like the researchers who worked on YoNAH, the SPLASH scientists want to know the size of the humpback population they are studying, the North Pacific humpbacks. They would like to know about how many humpbacks go to each of the winter and summer grounds and whether the whales from one group ever mate with the whales from another group. These researchers also want to know more about how various human activities affect the humpbacks. For example, they would like to know how often North Pacific humpbacks become entangled in fishing gear and how they have been affected by pollution in the ocean. SPLASH is the most thorough study of North Pacific humpbacks ever undertaken.[6]

Researchers who photograph humpbacks, take tissue samples, or study them in other ways usually work near a coastline. Some humpbacks spend a lot of their time away from a coast, however. This is true of a group of North Pacific humpbacks that

NOAA Ocean Explorer: Dr. Mate onboard the Beagle - Microsoft Internet Explorer

File   Edit   View   Favorites   Tools   Help

Address   http://oceanexplorer.noaa.gov/projects/02census/nekton/media/beagle.html   Go

...n State University's Dr. Bruce Mate and two research

The **Marine Nekton as Ocean Explorers Summary** includes results gained from a NOAA-funded study by Dr. Bruce Mate of Oregon State University to track the movements of humpbacks off Oregon and California. Dr. Mate and two research assistants are pictured aboard the *Beagle*.

spend the winter off Socorro Island, west of Mexico. Researchers have watched the whales near Socorro Island in the winter, but until recently, they did not know where the whales spent spring and summer.

Tracking Humpbacks With Satellite Tags

In February 2003, Dr. Bruce Mate of Oregon State University traveled to Socorro Island with a research team to attach electronic tags to the whales so that they could be monitored by satellite. To do this, Dr. Mate and his team went out in a boat and shot a tag into the skin of each whale with a crossbow. They tagged eleven whales in all.

Each satellite tag, small enough to fit in the palm of one's hand, sent signals to a satellite orbiting hundreds of miles above the earth. When the whale was under water, the tag, equipped with an antenna, collected information about where the whale was located. When the humpback and the tag were above the surface of the water, the tag transmitted a signal to the satellite when it orbited near the location of the whale. Special instruments on the satellite then transmitted the information on the whale's location to computers at Dr. Mate's laboratory in Oregon.

Dr. Mate and his team discovered that the whales migrated to the west coast of Canada and the southeast coast of Alaska. They knew that humpbacks from Hawaii visited these summer grounds, but they had no idea that humpbacks from Socorro Island were there, too. The Socorro Island humpbacks never stayed very close to any coastline, however, even after they arrived at their summer feeding ground.[7]

Scientists connected with the Indo-South Atlantic Consortium on Humpback Whales, or ISACH, have put satellite tags on some humpbacks that spend their winters near the coast of Gabon, in West Africa. They would like to know where in the Antarctic the humpbacks go in the spring.

To manage the whales' summer and winter grounds with as little disturbance as possible, conservationists need to know where the whales are.

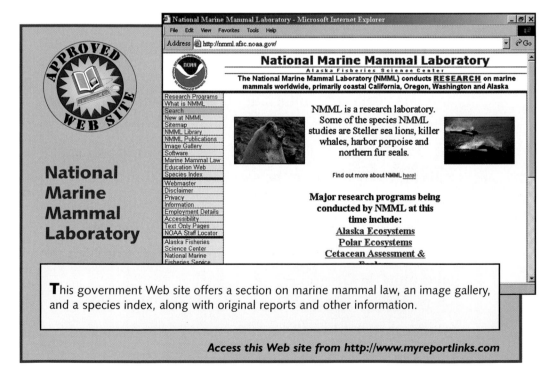

This government Web site offers a section on marine mammal law, an image gallery, and a species index, along with original reports and other information.

Access this Web site from http://www.myreportlinks.com

Researchers are still discovering the locations of some of these important habitats and the routes that the whales use to get there. Scientists are not sure that the whales experience pain when they are tagged, since some whales show no reaction. But most scientists believe that the information gained from monitoring the whales will benefit them in the long run and make up for any pain.

▶ Peregian, the Stranded Whale

Many conservation groups that study large populations of whales also get involved in other kinds of work. Some help save one whale at a time. On a sunny day in late winter, a humpback was swimming close to Peregian Beach, off the east coast of Australia. A couple of waves hit the whale, pushing it toward the beach. When the wave moved back to sea, the whale was still on the sand.

Some people tried to push the whale into the ocean, but that did not work. They reported the stranded whale to some authorities, who then contacted organizations that work with marine mammal strandings. While waiting for the rescue team, people along the beach covered the whale with sheets so that its skin would not dry out. They also formed a bucket brigade so that they could pour seawater on the whale to keep its temperature at a safe level.

In the morning, two excavators and other heavy equipment arrived on the beach. Some workers dug a channel leading to the ocean in front of the whale. Others built a wall on each side of the whale and left some space for the water to flow around it as the tide rose. By that time, there were thousands of people standing behind barricades. They had come to watch the operation, which was being filmed by television cameramen. A group of rescuers stood near the whale. Out on the ocean, a boat was waiting to pull the whale, named Peregian by his rescuers, out to sea.

As the tide rose and the water got closer to the whale, rescuers slipped a harness over the whale. The harness had a long rope attached to it that

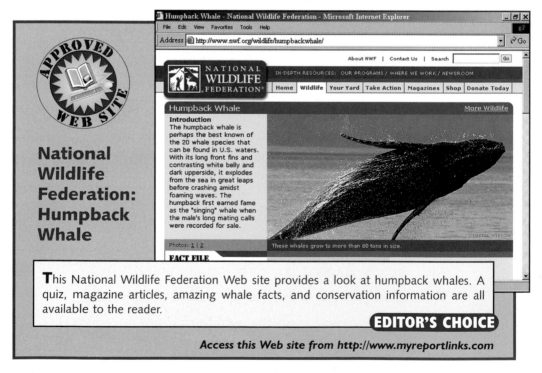

National Wildlife Federation: Humpback Whale

This National Wildlife Federation Web site provides a look at humpback whales. A quiz, magazine articles, amazing whale facts, and conservation information are all available to the reader.

EDITOR'S CHOICE

Access this Web site from http://www.myreportlinks.com

went all the way to the boat on the water. At high tide, rescuers pushed the whale while the boat pulled it into the ocean. Peregian slipped out of the harness and did what came naturally, swimming away while the rescuers and the crowd cheered and whistled.[8]

Researchers are not sure why whales become stranded. Strandings occur more often at beaches that slope very gently and have bars of sand running into the water, which may confuse the whales. Some researchers think that changes in the earth's magnetic field, which whales may use to guide them during migration, may confuse them.[9] According to a recent study conducted in Australia, wind patterns that affect the climate may cause strandings, too.[10] When whales become stranded, they are helpless and often die. Many countries, including Australia and the United States, have teams that can arrive on very short notice to attempt rescues.

Disentangling Whales

Humpbacks do not become stranded very often, but many become entangled in fishing gear. The Provincetown Center for Coastal Studies, PCCS, which is headquartered at the tip of Cape Cod, Massachusetts, has freed more than sixty large whales in the western North Atlantic and Gulf of Maine since 1984. This nonprofit conservation

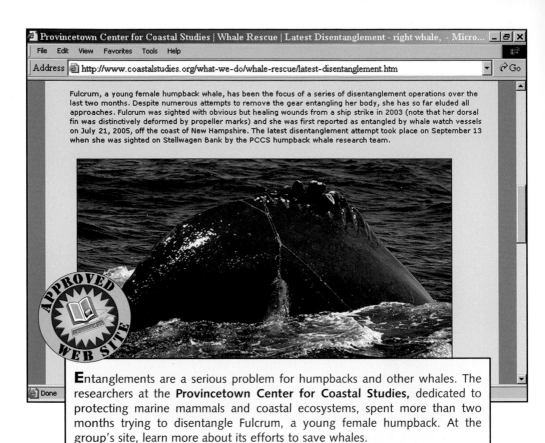

Provincetown Center for Coastal Studies | Whale Rescue | Latest Disentanglement - right whale, - Micro...

File   Edit   View   Favorites   Tools   Help

Address   http://www.coastalstudies.org/what-we-do/whale-rescue/latest-disentanglement.htm

Fulcrum, a young female humpback whale, has been the focus of a series of disentanglement operations over the last two months. Despite numerous attempts to remove the gear entangling her body, she has so far eluded all approaches. Fulcrum was sighted with obvious but healing wounds from a ship strike in 2003 (note that her dorsal fin was distinctively deformed by propeller marks) and she was first reported as entangled by whale watch vessels on July 21, 2005, off the coast of New Hampshire. The latest disentanglement attempt took place on September 13 when she was sighted on Stellwagen Bank by the PCCS humpback whale research team.

Entanglements are a serious problem for humpbacks and other whales. The researchers at the **Provincetown Center for Coastal Studies,** dedicated to protecting marine mammals and coastal ecosystems, spent more than two months trying to disentangle Fulcrum, a young female humpback. At the group's site, learn more about its efforts to save whales.

organization believes that trying to save every whale is important.

Humpbacks share their summer grounds with another large whale that is far more endangered than the humpback. It is the North Atlantic right whale, and there are fewer than four hundred left. About ten years ago, PCCS became the coordinator of a new disentanglement network to help humpbacks, right whales, and other entangled large whales.

The network helps whales that have become entangled in fishing gear anywhere along the east coast of the United States and the Canadian Maritime Provinces to the north. When someone reports that he or she has found an entangled whale, a first response team arrives as quickly as possible. There are teams ready to go into action at summer and winter feeding grounds and places where whales seem to become entangled often. The people on these teams are experienced at handling boats and marine mammals. Some are fishermen, who are often the first people to find an entangled whale.

First Response

The first responders will accurately describe the entanglement and stay with the whale until the main rescue team arrives. Sometimes the rescue team cannot come for a while or the sea may be too rough for a rescue. In that case, the first response team may attach a satellite tag to the fishing gear so that the Provincetown Center for Coastal Studies can keep track of the whale's location.

But not all entangled whales can or should be rescued. Rescuing an entangled whale is danger-ous work, and the decision to act is based on several factors: what kind of gear the whale is trapped in, how that gear is trapping the whale,

Whale Songs

Whale Songs - Microsoft Internet Explorer

File   Edit   View   Favorites   Tools   Help

Address http://www.whalesongs.org/

Ads by Goooooogle

Underwater Sounds
Listen to dolphins and whales with Cetacean Research hydrophones!
www.cetaceanresearch.c

Whale Watching
Private Luxury Yachts For Parties, Weddings & More; Affordable Rates!
www.urbandesirecruises.

Oahu Whale Watching
The Humpback Whales have returned to Hawaii. Snorkel & Scuba tours.
www.HawaiiActive.com

Whale Songs

A RESOURCE FOR TEACHERS, STUDENTS AND   WHALE LOVERS

Welcome to Whale Songs, an educational center about people, dolphins and whales. It is an evolving resource, encouraging communication among researchers, students, educators and whale lovers worldwide.

CETACEAN INFORMATION   CETACEAN NEWS   CETACEAN TRIVIA   LESSON PLANS   ABOUT "WHALE SONGS"

IN THE NEWS: Sun Jul 24th   Right whale deaths go unnoticed, report says
Fri Jul 22nd   Whale meat market expected to increase
Fri Jul 22nd   Scientists Challenge US Gov. to Enforce Endangered Species Act

International newspaper articles, newswire stories, and reports on whales can be found on this educational Web site. Learn about whales from the information presented and then take the Cetacean trivia quiz to test your knowledge.

Access this Web site from http://www.myreportlinks.com

and whether it will be safe for both the people trying to disentangle it and the whale itself. Whales that are trapped are already under a lot of stress, and most whales will not realize that humans are trying to help it. If the whale dives or slaps its tremendously strong tail on the water because it is frightened, the movement of this huge animal can injure a rescuer on the boat.

To avoid this situation, rescuers may try to tire the whale before they begin disentangling it. They do this by attaching floats to the fishing gear trailing from the whale. It is difficult for the whale to dive under water with the floats attached. The floats also add weight and make it harder for the whale to swim. Once the animal stops struggling and is almost still, the rescuers can try to cut it free from the fishing gear.[11]

But whales often do not wait for the rope to be cut—they may struggle and become even more injured than they were to begin with.

▶ Avoiding Whale Entanglements

Although conservation organizations like the PCCS get involved in emergency rescue work, it is not their main mission. They would rather find a way to prevent whale entanglements in the first place.

Large whales are not the only creatures in the sea that become entangled in fishing gear. Every year, millions of birds, turtles, dolphins, and other

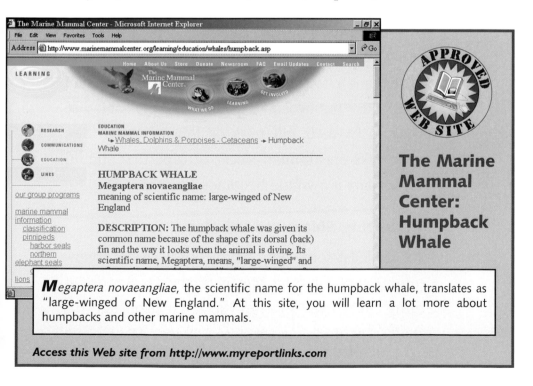

Megaptera novaeangliae, the scientific name for the humpback whale, translates as "large-winged of New England." At this site, you will learn a lot more about humpbacks and other marine mammals.

Access this Web site from http://www.myreportlinks.com

animals are accidentally caught in fishing gear all over the world and die as a result. This accidental catch is also referred to as an accidental "take" in the fishing community.

In the United States, the National Marine Fisheries Service (NMFS) is trying to do something about the problem. NMFS is a government agency charged with helping to protect the nation's marine life. To assist large whales in the Atlantic Ocean, NMFS organized a "take-reduction team." Conservationists, scientists, government agencies, and fishermen are working together to come up with ways to reduce the number of whale entanglements.

The take-reduction team will be releasing a plan in the near future. As a result of the team's earlier recommendations, NMFS has already made some changes in New England. Fishermen there must put weak links in the lines that are attached to their gill nets or lobster traps. The weak links are thinner pieces of rope that should break apart if a whale becomes entangled.[12]

▶ Separating Ships and Whales

With at least some help from conservation organizations, the National Marine Fisheries Service is trying to solve another serious problem for whales: collisions with large ships. Of all the human activities that go on in whale habitats,

NOAA Fisheries - National Marine Fisheries Service - Microsoft Internet Explorer

File   Edit   View   Favorites   Tools   Help

Address http://www.nmfs.noaa.gov/   Go

NOAA FISHERIES SERVICE

About Us | Regions | Science Centers | Councils | Commissions | Advisory Committee | Contact Us

Search   Go fish!

Welcome to NOAA's National Marine Fisheries Service (NOAA Fisheries Service). NOAA Fisheries Service is dedicated to the stewardship of living marine resources through science-based conservation and management, and the promotion of healthy ecosystems.

As a steward, NOAA Fisheries Service conserves, protects, and manages living marine resources in a way that ensures their continuation as functioning

Features
■ Magnuson-Stevens 2005
■ Bycatch
■ Grants
■ International Interests
■ Legislation
■ Pe...

Managing Marine Ecosystems
Sustaining Fisheries
Protecting Marine Species
Conserving Marine Habitat
Science & Technology
Law Enforcement

Administration & Operations
Constituent Services
Management & Budget
EEO & Diversity
Information Technology

National Marine Fisheries Service

The conservation and management of America's marine ecosystems is handled by NOAA's National Marine Fisheries Service. Learn more about this government agency's history, projects, and plans from its Web site.

Access this Web site from http://www.myreportlinks.com

shipping is one of the most dangerous. In 2004, two pregnant female North Atlantic right whales were struck by ships along the mid-Atlantic coast. The deaths of pregnant females are especially tragic when a whale population is as endangered as the right whale population is.

After years of consulting with shipping companies, scientists, and conservationists, NMFS announced that it will be putting a plan into effect. The plan will separate ships and whales as much as possible in the most dangerous places for whales, at the most dangerous times of year, such as migration. The plan is designed with North Atlantic right whales in mind because there are so few of them. Humpbacks share some feeding grounds with right whales in spring and summer, so there is hope that the plan will help them, too.

During spring, ships will avoid Cape Cod Bay, which is south of Stellwagen Bank, as much as possible. The bay is an important feeding ground for right whales. There will also be new safety rules for ships going through the Great South

▲ If humpbacks like this one are to survive, whale collisions, entanglements, and other threats will need to be addressed by the governments of the world.

Channel. The channel is part of a busy shipping lane between New York and Boston. Humpbacks feed there and in Cape Cod Bay along with right whales.

When it is not possible to separate ships and whales, some researchers and conservationists believe that ships need to travel more slowly in the North Atlantic when they are near whale populations. Researchers fear that collisions with whales are often not reported by a ship's crew, so they believe that there are even more accidents than anyone knows about. In the summer of 2005, conservationists urged the United States government to take action.[13] Although researchers are especially worried about North Atlantic right whales, slower ships mean humpback lives will be saved, too.

Watching Out for Whales

Whale-watching boats are usually not a danger to whales, but in some regions, there may be too many boats. About one million people take whale-watching cruises to the Stellwagen Bank National Marine Sanctuary each year. In the late 1990s, a couple of the whale-watching boats accidentally hit whales.

In January 1999, the Provincetown Center for Coastal Studies and the Stellwagen Bank sanctuary organized a public discussion on how to manage whale watching to ensure the whales' safety. The discussion was led by a panel of eighteen experts including the operators of whale-watching boats, scientists, conservationists, and representatives of NMFS. Many members of the panel were concerned about the number of boats that were operating in the Stellwagen sanctuary and what effect those vessels have on whale behavior.

After the discussion, another group of experts sponsored by the NMFS met to draft guidelines for whale-watching-boat operators. The guidelines limit the speed of boats within 2 miles (3 kilometers) of a whale. They also limit the amount of time and the number of boats that can be near a whale. In Hawaii, no boat is allowed to approach a whale within 100 yards (91 meters) of the animal. In New England, it is suggested that no boat approach within 100 feet (30 meters) and that there be no more than one boat at a time within 100 yards (91 meters).[14]

Speaking Out for Whales in Australia

Conservation organizations in other parts of the world speak out publicly to help whales and other marine mammals, too. The Whale and Dolphin Conservation Society (WDCS), a global organization based in England, has urged the Australian government to get rid of shark nets. These nets are set up near public beaches for the protection of

The mission of the Whale and Dolphin Conservation Society is to reduce and ultimately eliminate threats to the world's whales, dolphins, and porpoises. Learn more about this charitable organization at its Web site, which also provides information on humpback whale migration, distribution, and the problems the species faces.

EDITOR'S CHOICE

Access this Web site from http://www.myreportlinks.com

swimmers when sharks are a problem. WDCS feels that the nets do not do a very good job of keeping sharks off the beaches, and thousands of marine animals have become entangled in the nets, including at least one humpback.

The WDCS is also urging the Australian government to adopt a marine mammal protection act like the one in the United States. Australia has more than forty species of whales and dolphins, and five are in danger of becoming extinct.

THE FUTURE OF THE WORLD'S HUMPBACKS

Starting in the 1970s, a global conservation movement to preserve the earth helped preserve the humpbacks, too. People discovered what truly magnificent creatures these whales were. They could even sing!

Many countries, including the United States, realized that humpbacks and other great whales were in serious danger of becoming extinct. The United States passed some strong laws to help them, including the Endangered Species Act and the Marine Mammal Protection Act. The International Whaling Commission's moratorium on whaling also helped save humpbacks.

These enormous acrobats of the ocean seem to be recovering well now that so few of them are hunted. Conservationists, scientists, and whale lovers still worry about the humpback's future, though, for a number of reasons.

▶ The End of the Whaling Moratorium?

There is a chance that the International Whaling Commission will end its moratorium on whaling,

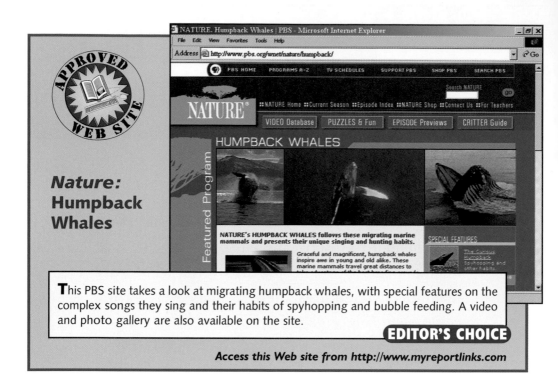

Nature: Humpback Whales

HUMPBACK WHALES

NATURE's HUMPBACK WHALES follows these migrating marine mammals and presents their unique singing and hunting habits.

Graceful and magnificent, humpback whales inspire awe in young and old alike. These marine mammals travel great distances to

This PBS site takes a look at migrating humpback whales, with special features on the complex songs they sing and their habits of spyhopping and bubble feeding. A video and photo gallery are also available on the site.

EDITOR'S CHOICE

Access this Web site from http://www.myreportlinks.com

although the IWC is going through great changes at the moment. Its voting members seem to be split on the question of ending the ban on whaling. Three quarters of the membership must vote in favor of lifting the moratorium to overturn the ban, and most conservationists think that is unlikely to happen in the next few years.[1]

For the past decade, some members of the IWC have been trying to come up with a new plan for managing commercial whaling. They call it the Revised Management Scheme (RMS). Countries in favor of whaling think that with a good plan in place, the populations of humpbacks and other whales can remain stable when commercial whaling begins again.

Some IWC members believe that the moratorium cannot remain in place forever because too many countries want to begin commercial whaling again. They think that the best way to protect humpbacks is to create a strong management scheme that will make cheating difficult. The United States belongs to this group. It believes that the management scheme will be stronger if the IWC gets rid of scientific permits, which some countries have used for commercial whaling instead of serious research.

Opposition to the Scheme

Many countries that are against whaling, however, are also against the new management scheme. They argue that it does not give the IWC a way to enforce its own rules. They believe that when whaling resumes, some countries will lie about the number of whales they kill and exceed the number of whales they are allowed to hunt. If that happens, humpbacks and other whales will be in danger once again. And it may not be in a country's best financial interest to resume commercial whaling, in any case. The Whale and Dolphin Conservation Society likes to point out that whale appreciation, rather than whale slaughter, can contribute a lot of money to a nation's economy. In 1998, people spent almost $33 million on whale-watching tours in Japan, $12 million in Norway, and $357 million in the United States.[2]

Preserving the Earth and Saving the Whales

Commercial whaling is a threat to the humpback's future, but it is not the only one. Collisions between whales and ships are a problem for humpbacks. So are entanglements in fishing equipment. You may think that you cannot do much to help solve these problems, but you can play a very important role in helping to fight global warming.

Our planet seems to be warming gradually as a result of the rising levels of carbon dioxide in our atmosphere. The temperature of the ocean around Antarctica has risen 2 percent in the last fifty years. Ninety percent of the world's large whales feed in Antarctica, including thousands of humpbacks.[3] Researchers are not sure exactly how the warming oceans will affect the whales. When the ice shelves melt, the ocean will not be as salty, and that is sure to have some effect on the creatures that make the world's seas their home.

Less Is More

More research is needed on how global warming will affect whales and other living things. But we can all do our part to reduce the amount of carbon dioxide in the atmosphere. If we all use less energy

▲ *The future of humpbacks and all other animals on earth depends on us.*

in our cars, our homes, and our factories, there will be less carbon dioxide in the air to trap the sun's rays. By going on an "energy diet," we may be helping to save the humpbacks and preserve the entire web of life on our planet.

▶ Become a Whale Activist

You may decide that you would like to influence the people and organizations with the most direct power to help humpbacks and other whales. Letters can be very effective. Write your U.S. senators and congressmen and tell them that you would like the National Marine Fisheries Service to do more to help whales, such as forcing ships traveling near whales to slow down. You can also write directly to the International Whaling Commission to say that you do not want the commission to end the moratorium on hunting whales. You can even write to the President of the United States and urge him to sign the Kyoto Protocol, so that the United States does its part to cut down on global warming. If you want your letters to have a bigger impact, think about organizing a letter-writing campaign and get your friends and family to write some letters, too.

Humpbacks and other whales have been in our oceans for millions of years. We humans are more recent arrivals on Planet Earth, but occasionally, we think of the ocean as our own watery highway, to use as we please. It would be nice if we could all learn to "share the road"!

In 1973, Congress took the farsighted step of creating the Endangered Species Act, widely regarded as the world's strongest and most effective wildlife conservation law. It set an ambitious goal: to reverse the alarming trend of human-caused extinction that threatened the ecosystems we all share.

Each book in this series explores the life of an endangered animal. The books tell how and why the animals have become endangered and explain the efforts being made to restore their populations.

The United States Fish and Wildlife Service and the National Marine Fisheries Service share responsibility for administration of the Endangered Species Act. Over time, animals are added to, reclassified in, or removed from the federal list of Endangered and Threatened Wildlife and Plants. At the time of publication, all the animals in this series were listed as endangered species. The most up-to-date list can be found at **http://www.fws.gov/endangered/wildlife.html**.

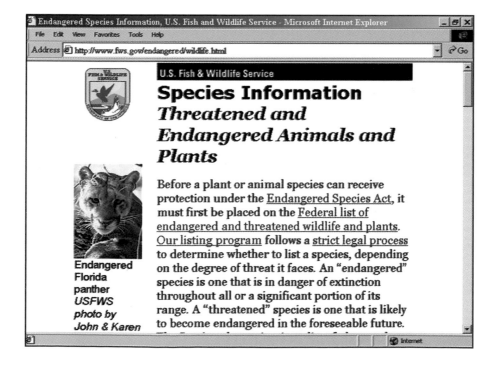

		STOP					
Back	Forward	Stop	Review	Home	Explore	Favorites	History

Report Links

The Internet sites described below can be accessed at http://www.myreportlinks.com

▶**National Wildlife Federation: Humpback Whale**
Editor's Choice Learn about humpbacks at this National Wildlife Federation Web site.

▶**Whales and Dolphins—Humpback Whales**
Editor's Choice For the latest news on humpbacks, visit this World Wildlife Fund Web site.

▶**Stellwagen Bank National Marine Sanctuary**
Editor's Choice Visit this whale-friendly sanctuary located in Massachusetts.

▶**Whale Center of New England**
Editor's Choice The Whale Center of New England specializes in field-based whale research.

▶**Whale and Dolphin Conservation Society: Humpback Whale**
Editor's Choice The Whale and Dolphin Conservation Society protects cetaceans.

▶***Nature*: Humpback Whales**
Editor's Choice This Web site offers an overview of the "curious" humpback whale.

▶**American Cetacean Society**
At this site, learn how marine scientists build bridges with the public to protect marine species.

▶**Baleen Whales**
SeaWorld offers an overview of baleen whales on this site.

▶**Cetacea**
This site provides information on whales and related species.

▶**Greenpeace International**
Learn about an organization trying to save our fragile earth.

▶**Hawaii Humpback Study**
Read the Pacific Whale Foundation's humpback whale study.

▶**Hawaiian Islands Humpback Whale National Marine Sanctuary**
Find out about a safe haven for humpback whales in Hawaii.

▶**The International Whaling Commission**
Learn about the International Whaling Commission from its Web site.

▶**The Marine Mammal Center: Humpback Whale**
The Marine Mammal Center offers information about humpbacks and other marine mammals.

▶**Marine Nekton as Ocean Explorers Summary**
Learn how scientists use satellites to track the location of North Pacific humpback whales.

Report Links

The Internet sites described below can be accessed at
http://www.myreportlinks.com

▶**Modern Whaling**
A brief history of modern whaling is presented at this site.

▶**Monterey Bay National Marine Sanctuary**
Visit this national marine sanctuary's site and find out how humpback whales are protected.

▶**National Marine Fisheries Service**
Information on the government's role in ocean management and conservation is available here.

▶**National Marine Mammal Laboratory**
View the latest research on marine mammals from this government site.

▶**National Marine Sanctuaries**
This Web site highlights the history and importance of the nation's marine sanctuaries.

▶**New Bedford Whaling Museum**
Visit the virtual home of the largest whaling museum in the United States.

▶**NSW National Parks and Wildlife Service: Humpback Whale**
This Australian Web site presents information on whales and other endangered animals.

▶**Ocean Alliance**
Learn about the state of the world's oceans from this Web site.

▶**The Oceania Project**
This organization is dedicated to raising awareness about whales and related species.

▶**Provincetown Center for Coastal Studies**
A nonprofit works to save marine life in New England.

▶**Species At Risk: Humpback Whale**
The North Pacific population of humpbacks is highlighted on this Canadian Web page.

▶**USFWS Endangered Species Program Kids Corner**
This USFWS Web site offers ways you can help save endangered species.

▶**The Voyage of the *Odyssey***
Learn about an epic scientific journey to study the effects of ocean pollution on marine species.

▶**Whale Songs**
This Web site educates people about whales and other related species.

▶**Whaling and Fishing**
This academic Web site offers information on the effects of modern whaling on whale species.

baleen—Hundreds of pairs of baleen plates hang from the roof of the mouth of some whales, including humpbacks, to help them filter their food. They are made of keratin, just like your fingernails. Each baleen plate has a fringe that faces inward, toward the whale's throat, to catch its food.

blowhole—The hole at the top of a whale's head through which the whale breathes. Humpbacks have two blowholes, like all baleen whales.

breach—(noun) A whale's leap out of the water; (verb) to leap from the water.

bubble netting—A feeding technique in which whales swim upward while blowing bubbles that trap fish and krill.

buoy—A colorful marker made out of wood or Styrofoam that floats on the water. Buoys help fishermen find their crab or lobster traps.

Cetacea—This large order or group of marine mammals comprises eighty species of whales, including the humpback, as well as dolphins and porpoises.

conservationist—Someone who tries to preserve the earth's natural resources and its wildlife, including whales.

dorsal—Refers to an animal part situated near or on its back; humpback whales have a dorsal fin.

emissions—Substances released into the air, such as exhaust from a car's engine.

extinct—No longer alive or in existence, such as a species of plant or animal.

flukes—The two identical parts of a whale's tail.

global warming—A rise in temperature of the earth's air and oceans as a result of pollution in the earth's atmosphere. The pollution comes from a combination of greenhouse gases, including carbon dioxide, produced by human activities such as driving cars.

involuntary—Reflexive, or not controlled by will.

longlines—Very long fishing lines that can stretch for dozens of miles and are baited with hundreds of hooks.

lunge feeding—A way in which humpbacks feed as a group by swimming into a mass of fish and krill with their mouths open, taking in great amounts of water and then expelling it.

marine—Related to the ocean. A marine mammal is a mammal that lives in the ocean.

migration—A move from one region to another. Whales migrate twice a year, in spring and late fall.

moratorium—The complete, but temporary, stop of an activity, such as whaling.

national marine sanctuary—A marine area, such as a gulf or bay, that is protected by the United States government to conserve wildlife and habitat.

petroleum—A thick, oily liquid that lies below the earth's surface in some parts of the world. It is used to make gasoline and heating oil.

piscivore—An animal that eats fish.

pollution—Materials that harm the earth's air, water, and soil. *Pollution* also refers to the act of harming the earth.

quota—A fixed number that represents a share; in the case of whaling, it represents the maximum number of whales that can be killed in a given period.

rorqual—A small family of whales within the larger group of baleen whales. A rorqual has a lot of deep grooves in its throat. These grooves expand like the folds of an accordion when the whale takes a gulp of seawater.

spyhopping—A behavior in which humpbacks poke their heads out of the water and often turn around, as if to spy on other creatures, including humans.

synthetic—Something that is produced by people rather than found in nature, such as a synthetic chemical.

traplines—Long lines that connect traps, such as lobster traps, which float in a circuit or arch.

whaler—A person who hunts whales.

Chapter 1. Humpbacks Need Our Help

1. "Geared Up and Going Nowhere," *Alaska,* vol. 67, no. 8., October 1, 2001, p. 10.

2. "Humpback Whale," *American Cetacean Society Fact Sheet,* n.d., <www.acsonline.org/factpack/humpback.htm> (May 4, 2005).

3. Roger Payne, *Among Whales* (New York: Scribner, 1995), p. 269.

4. "Frequently Asked Questions," *Provincetown Center for Coastal Studies,* n.d., <www.coastalstudies.org/what-we-do/whale-rescue/faq.htm> (April 13, 2005).

Chapter 2. The Giant Singer of the Sea

1. "Symphony of the Deep," from National Public Radio's Radio Expeditions, n.d., <www.nationalgeographic.com/radiox/humpback/hw_archive.html> (May 13, 2005).

2. Roger Payne, *Among Whales* (New York: Scribner, 1995), p. 144.

3. Mark Simmonds, *Whales and Dolphins of the World* (Cambridge: MIT Press, 2004), p. 15.

4. Payne, p. 142.

5. Stephen Martin, *The Whales' Journey* (Crows Nest, Australia: Allen & Unwin, 2001), p. 39.

6. Simmonds, p. 72.

7. Ibid., p. 68.

8. Martin, p. 48.

9. Ibid., p. 45.

10. Ibid., p. 32.

11. "Where Else in the World Are Humpback Whales Found?" *Whale and Dolphin Conservation Society,* n.d., <http://www.wdcs.org/dan/publishing.nsf/allweb/776C09B914E6D84580256C53002F9988> (April 29, 2005).

12. Payne, p. 152.

13. Martin, p. 96.

14. "Humpback Whale," *The Marine Mammal Center,* n.d., <www.marinemammalcenter.org/learning/education/whales/humpback.asp> (April 28, 2005).

15. Payne, p. 38.

16. Michael Tennesen, "Tuning In to Humpback Whales," *National Wildlife,* February/March 2002, vol. 40, no. 2, <www.nwf.org/nationawildlife/article.cfm?articleId=444&issueId=40> (August 18, 2005).

17. Payne, p. 158.

18. Martin, p. 181.

Chapter 3. How Humans Have Harmed Whales

1. Mark Simmonds, *Whales and Dolphins of the World* (Cambridge: MIT Press, 2004), p. 102.

2. Stephen Martin, *The Whales' Journey* (Crows Nest, Australia: Allen & Unwin, 2001), p. 9.

3. Simmonds, p. 121.

4. Ibid., p. 122.

5. "Scientists Prepare for Humpbacks' Survival," *Whale and Dolphin Conservation Society,* March 1, 1999, <www.wdcs.org/dan/publishing/nsf/allweb/DA0ADDD80B99DD4780256D0300519> (April 30, 2005).

6. "Conservation and the Whale Center," *Whale Center of New England,* n.d., <www.whalecenter.org/conservation/conservation.htm> (May 2, 2005).

7. "Generalized diagram of a gillnet," *Provincetown Center for Coastal Studies,* n.d., <www.coastalstudies.org/what-we-do/whale-rescue/gillnet.htm> (April 27, 2005).

8. Roger Payne, *Among Whales* (New York: Scribner, 1995), p. 304.

9. "Welcome to the PCB Home Page at EPA," U.S. Environmental Protection Agency, n.d., <www.epa.gov/opptintr/pcb/> (May 24, 2005).

10. "What's the Problem? Why Loud Sound Is a Problem in the Ocean," *American Cetacean Society*, n.d., <www.acsonline.org/issues/sound/sound-primer/problem.html> (May 4, 2005).

11. "Whale Deaths from Ship Collisions Up," *Whale and Dolphin Conservation Society*, April 22, 2002, <www.wdcs.org/dan/publishing.nsf/allweb/88D1EFB0E35FACEA80256D0300517F> (April 30, 2005).

12. "Arctic Ice Shelf Splits," *BBC News World Edition*, Tuesday, September 23, 2003, <news.bbc.co.uk/2/hi/science/nature/3132074.stm> (May 25, 2005).

Chapter 4. The Struggle to Save Humpbacks and Other Whales

1. David Day, *The Whale War* (San Francisco: Sierra Club Books, 1987), pp. 11–12.

2. Roger Payne, *Among Whales* (New York: Scribner, 1995), p. 299.

3. Day, p. 29.

4. Ibid., pp. 96, 98–99.

5. Payne, p. 296.

6. Ibid., p. 269.

7. "Humpback Whale," *American Cetacean Society*, n.d., <www.acsonline.org/factpack/humpback.htm> (May 4, 2005).

8. "Humpback Breeding Ground," *Provincetown Center for Coastal Studies*, n.d., <www.coastalstudies.org/what-we-do/education-programs/whale-watching/large-whales/humpbackbreeding-research.html> (May 29, 2005).

9. Mark Simmonds, *Whales and Dolphins of the World* (Cambridge: MIT Press, 2004), p. 140; "*Megaptera novaeangliae*," *The IUCN Red List of Threatened Species*, 2003, <www.redlist.org/search/details/php?species=13006> (May 20, 2005).

10. Simmonds, p. 143.

Chapter 5. What Scientists and Conservationists Are Doing

1. Barbara Taormina, "75 Humpbacks Are Christened at Conference," *Gloucester Daily Times,* March 30, 2001, <www.whalecenter.org/conservation/gdteg301.htm> (May 2, 2005).

2. Mason T. Weinrich, *Observations: The Humpback Whales of Stellwagen Bank* (Gloucester, Mass.: Whale Research Press, 1983), p. 51.

3. "Humpback Season Underway at PCCS," *Provincetown Center for Coastal Studies,* April 20, 2005, <http://www.coastalstudies.org/whats-new/4-20-2005.htm> (April 28, 2005).

4. Stephen Martin, *The Whales' Journey* (Crows Nest, Australia: Allen & Unwin, 2001), p. 228.

5. "Years of the North Atlantic Humpbacks (YoNAH)," *Provincetown Center for Coastal Studies,* n.d., <www.coastalstudies.org/what-we-do/humpback-whales/years-of-humpback-whale.htm> (January 9, 2005).

6. "Biopsy Sampling," "Human Impacts," and "General Information," n.d., *SPLASH Hawaiian Islands Humpback Whale National Marine Sanctuary,* <hawaiihumpbackwhale.noaa.gov/special_offerings/sp_off/splash_general.html> (April 30, 2005).

7. "Humpback Whales: Socorro Island, Mexico," *Marine Mammal Program, Oregon State University,* n.d., <oregonstate.edu/groups/marinemammal/current%20research.htm> (April 20, 2005); "How Satellite Tags Work" and "How Satellite Tags Are Attached," *WhaleNet,* n.d., <whale.wheelock.edu/whalenet-stuff/sat_tags_work.html> (June 5, 2005).

8. Martin, pp. 218–221.

9. Ibid., p. 96.

10. "Whales and Weather," The *New York Times,* May 24, 2005.

11. "Introduction," *Provincetown Center for Coastal Studies,* n.d., <www.coastalstudies.org/whatwe-do/whale-rescue/introduction.htm> (April 27, 2005).

12. Barbara Taormina, "For This Tourist, a Grisly Fate," *Gloucester Daily Times,* April 18, 2001, <www.whalecenter.org/conservation/gdtinland401.htm> (June 5, 2005).

13. "Deaths of Rare Whales May Be Underreported, Scientists Say," The *New York Times,* July 24, 2005, <http://www.nytimes.com/2005/07/24/science/earth/24whale.html?ei=5070&en=48aca6f48e269d9e&ex=1122955200&adxnnl=1&emc=eta1&adxnnlx=1122471032-hxMKTkxBTLxmHLKVA6sgNQ> (August 18, 2005).

14. "Whale Watching Guidelines," *Provincetown Center for Coastal Studies,* n.d., <www.coastalstudies.org/whatwe-do/public-policy/whale-watching-guidelines.htm> (April 27, 2005).

Chapter 6. The Future of the World's Humpbacks

1. Phone conversation with Kate Sardi, assistant director of the Whale Center of New England, June 30, 2005.

2. "There Are Benign Alternatives to Whaling," *Whale and Dolphin Conservation Society,* n.d., <www.wdcs.org/dan/publishing.nsf/allweb/F3FB05626775072880256F35004A0D3F> (June 6, 2005).

3. "Introduction to Climate Change," *Whale and Dolphin Conservation Society,* n.d., <www.wdcs.org/dan/publishing.nsf/allweb/1BAE552DE9F85F1280256F2D005838A2> (June 6, 2005).

Collard, Sneed B. *A Whale Biologist at Work*. New York: Franklin Watts, 2001.

Currie, Stephen. *Thar She Blows: American Whaling in the Nineteenth Century*. Minneapolis: Lerner Publications, 2001.

Gentle, Victor, and Janet Perry. *Humpback Whales*. Milwaukee: Gareth Stevens, 2001.

Greenberg, Dan. *Whales*. New York: Benchmark Books, 2003.

Hirschmann, Kristine. *Humpback Whales*. San Diego: Kidhaven Press, 2003.

Jenner, Caryn. *The Journey of a Humpback Whale*. New York: Dorling Kindersley, 2002.

MacMillan, Diane M. *Humpback Whales*. Minneapolis: Carolrhoda Books, 2004.

Parks, Peggy J. *Global Warming*. San Diego: Kidhaven Press, 2004.

Philbrick, Nathaniel. *Revenge of the Whale: The True Story of the Whaleship* Essex. New York: G. P. Putnam, 2002.

Puay, Lim Cheng. *Our Warming Planet*. Chicago: Raintree, 2004.